CLASSIC
BUS

YEARBOOK – 9
Edited by Gavin Booth

Ian Allan
PUBLISHING

CONTENTS

3 INTRODUCTION

4 THE BRIGHTON ROAD
MICHAEL H C BAKER remembers trips to
the seaside and the buses he found when
he got there

16 CHECKPOINT/1
ALAN MILLAR checks out Exeter Corporation
Transport in the first of four Checkpoint pages

17 THREE IN A ROW
Artist, CHRIS DREW, takes triple-number
registrations as his running theme. This time
he finds buses with 000 and 111 numbers

18 THE GAME OF THE NAME
Names for types of bus and coach are usually
easier to remember than numbers, says
GAVIN BOOTH – with the emphasis on
'usually'. Here he offers an informal history of
named chassis

28 CLASSIC WONDERBUS
In the antidote to his regular Blunderbus articles
in *Classic Bus* magazine, ALAN MILLAR turns his
attention to the single-decker that was 'by far
the best of its generation'

31 THREE IN A ROW
In his second selection, CHRIS DREW focuses
on 222 and 333

32 WE ARE NOT WORTHY
GAVIN BOOTH pays reluctant homage to the
Routemaster as an introduction to
GEOFF RIXON's colour pictures on the next
eight pages

41 THE FIRST FLEETLINES
It was the model that brought Daimlers into
a wide selection of fleets. GEOFF O'BRIEN
pictures recall early versions of the famous
rear-engined chassis

45 ON OTHER PAGES
Colour photographs linking with the articles in
this book – Brighton, Bristol REs, CIÉ's M-class
Leopards, South Wales, Economic and Trent

49 CHECKPOINT/2
CIÉ's distinctive M-class Leopards get the
ALAN MILLAR once-over

50 COACHBUILDING IN BRIDLINGTON
Blackpool, yes. Hove, yes. Scarborough, yes.
But Bridlington? MIKE FENTON explains how
a yachtbuilder turned to coachbuilding

61 A 40-YEAR LOVE-AFFAIR
Before it became obsessed with Leylands,
Edinburgh Corporation enjoyed a long and
fruitful association with Daimlers.
GAVIN BOOTH tells the story

73 THREE IN A ROW
For its third outing, CHRIS DREW turns to 444
and 555

74 THE ECONOMIC BUS SERVICE
In a major article, GEOFF BURROWS provides an
account of one of the pioneering bus operations
in the north-east of England

88 CHECKPOINT/3
The much-missed coachbuilder Eastern Coach
Works gets the Checkpoint treatment from
ALAN MILLAR

89 THE LAST THING ON MY MIND
If it's a ROBERT E JOWITT article, you might
think the last thing on his mind would be buses,
and you could be right. But his South Wales
pursuits don't necessarily involve the fair sex –
well, not all the time, anyway

100 THREE IN A ROW
CHRIS DREW reaches 666 – oh dear – and 777

101 TITANS TAKE OVER
COLIN ROUTH describes West Yorkshire's fleet
of Leyland TD1s and TD2s, supported by some
excellent contemporary photographs

111 CHECKPOINT/4
ALAN MILLAR turns his attention to the Trent
company

112 THE WAY THINGS WERE
Photos taken by JOHN ROBINSON 30 years ago

120 THREE IN A ROW
CHRIS DREW draws 888 and 999 to reach the
last of his three-figure selections

121 ROGER AND OUT
Regular *Classic Bus* columnist ROGER DAVIES
learns his As, Bs and Cs in 1960s Sheffield

First published 2003

ISBN 0 7110 2939 3

Design by Hieroglyph

Published by Ian Allan Publishing

An imprint of Ian Allan Publishing Ltd, Hersham, Surrey KT12 4RG

Printed by Ian Allan Printing Ltd, Hersham, Surrey KT12 4RG

Code: 0304/C2

INTRODUCTION

WHAT IS a classic bus – a question I am often asked; when you edit a bi-monthly magazine with that name, such questions are probably inevitable. In terms of the magazine's remit, a classic bus is one built more than 20 years ago, which normally means buses that are no longer in service, though the longevity of buses like London's Routemasters and some surprising survivors among fleets of all sizes means that 'classic' buses can still be in service.

I have applied the same definition to this ninth *Classic Bus Yearbook*, and although theoretically the first Leyland Olympian double-deckers could be covered – and no doubt they will be before long – we have spread our net to cover buses built over a broad period from the 1920s to the 1970s.

Of course our catch-all definition means that not all of the buses we cover have been entirely successful; 'classic' defines when they were built rather than how good they were. Over the past 10-plus years, our regular magazine columnist, Alan Millar, has found more than 60 types that fall into his Classic Blunderbus category – though he is quick to point out when readers write in to protest when their favourite bus appears in the Blunderbus column, that the label doesn't necessarily mean that they were bad buses – often they were the right bus at the wrong time. To avoid any such controversy, Alan nominates a Wonderbus in each Yearbook, and this time he has chosen one that few will surely disagree with.

Another regular contributor to the pages of the magazine is our tame sage, Geoff Burrows, who takes a break from wrestling with readers' queries for his Q&A column to present a fascinating history of and independent from his home patch, Economic Bus Service.

Elsewhere, Michael Baker recalls trips to Brighton and what he found there in The Brighton Road; Mike Fenton looks at a Bridlington yachtbuilder that got involved in bus bodies; Robert E Jowitt supplies one of his distinctive essays that combine his love of buses with his, er, other enthusiasms; Colin Routh recalls the Leyland Titan TD1s and TD2s bought by West Yorkshire Road Car before it moved on to a diet of Bristols; John Robinson remembers 1973 with some of his photographs; and I look at the names chosen by chassis manufacturers for their products, and at Edinburgh's Daimler legacy.

Full-colour features cover the London Routemaster, undeniably a classic, and the Daimler Fleetline, again a type that has a deservedly faithful following.

Regular features from the magazine are Checkpoint, where Alan Millar provides a thumbnail sketch of four bus-related topics, and Roger Davies contributes one of his characteristic Roger and Out sign-off pieces. Chris Drew, who supplies excellent line drawings for the magazine on London topics, casts his net wider as he draws buses with three-figure registrations.

Classic Bus magazine uses the strapline 'Remembering buses the way they used to be', and if that appeals to you and you enjoy this book, why not try the magazine as well?

Gavin Booth
Edinburgh

Front cover: *On pages 33-40 we celebrate that amazing survivor, the London Transport Routemaster, with Geoff Rixon colour photos of RMs in some of the more colourful liveries they have worn in London service. The cover photo shows London & Country no.4109, the former RM1183, at Cromwell Road, Kingston, on the 406 route in May 1994. The traditional Routemaster design suits the modern Ray Stenning L&C livery application.*
Geoff Rixon

Back cover, upper: *The Daimler Fleetline is also celebrated in colour, on pages 41-44. This 1962 Manchester Corporation Fleetline CRG6 with Metro-Cammell body is seen in Oldham on the 82 route in Greater Manchester PTE days, in August 1974.*
Gavin Booth

Back cover, lower: *Alan Millar nominates the Bristol RE as a Classic Wonderbus on pages 28-30. This 1972 RESL6L with ECW body, no.358 in the Ribble fleet, leaves Preston's distinctive bus station for Blackburn in May 1984.*
Gavin Booth

THE BRIGH

MICHAEL H C BAKER on trips to the seaside

ONE OF THE BIGGEST events in the
preservation year is the annual Historic
Commercial Vehicle Society (HCVS) run to
Brighton. It's been around a long time, 42 years to be
precise. The 53 miles between London and Brighton
is a nice convenient distance for any group wishing
to stage a race or a commemorative event and to be
able to start in the capital and finish beside the sea at
Britain's most cosmopolitan and oldest resort has
proved an irresistible lure since long before the days
of mechanised transport. In the boom years of the
early 19th century after the defeat of Napoleon, when
John Nash completed his extraordinary Royal
Pavilion and the court was regularly in residence, no
fewer than 52 stage coaches competed for business on
the Brighton road and the overall journey time had
come down to around three-and-a-half hours. Young
bucks raced each other, changing horses several
times. It was quite possible to return to the capital the
same evening; the day trip to the seaside had arrived.

My first visit to Brighton was a little later than
this, but well before the first HCVS run – the summer
of 1946 to be precise. The original London to
Brighton road, the A23, started at Westminster
Bridge, passed through South London, on through
Croydon, out into the country at Purley and
continued through Redhill and over the Surrey
border into Sussex at Crawley. It passed nowhere else
of great significance, although the countryside
looked delightful, until Brighton was reached. There
were important market towns to the east and west,
notably Haywards Heath and Horsham; alternative
routes between London and Brighton accommodated
them and when the main railway line was built it
passed through Haywards Heath. This line has always
been extremely busy and was electrified in 1933.
Nevertheless road congestion was becoming a real
problem at this time and in the 1930s the Croydon
bypass, or Purley Way, was built which not only kept
through traffic out of the ancient market town and

Left: *On the A23 at Pyecombe, Brighton-bound, in 1963, Southdown Leyland Titan PD2/12 no.788 with attractive Beadle body. The man on the central reservation provides a clue that this is the day of the annual HCVC London-Brighton run.* Michael Dryhurst

Below: *London Transport and Southdown met in Crawley and in the bus station are Southdown East Lancs-bodied Leyland Titan PD2/12 no.790 and London Transport RF106 on Green Line duties.* Michael Dryhurst

one-time summer residence of the Archbishops of Canterbury but also served its aerodrome which was then the official London Airport.

The bypass left the original road at Thornton Heath Pond and rejoined it at Purley. We lived two roads beyond the pond; at one end was London Road, the original Brighton Road, and at the other the new one, Purley Way (although just to confuse the issue at this point it was called Thornton Road – however you don't need to remember that as a question on it will not be included in the test at the end of this piece).

Daily service

Southdown provided a daily service from Victoria Coach Station to Brighton, which called, by prior arrangement, at the pond. At two-and-three-quarter hours with various stops including a refreshment one at Southdown's own buffet at County Oak, Crawley, this was only three-quarters-of-an-hour faster than a post-chaise managed in the 1820s, although non-stop coaches did the journey in two hours. War conditions brought about the withdrawal of all Southdown express services in 1942, but they started up again in the spring of 1946 and the handsome apple/dark-green-and-cream-liveried Leyland Tigers soon became a familiar sight making their elegant way southwards, easing past the Feltham, ex-LCC and former Croydon Corporation trams, overtaking gasping, archaic-looking ST double-deckers inherited from the LGOC and now in their late teens and long past their prime, which terminated beside the pond's hardly crystal-clear waters.

London Road was still the main artery for local traffic and was served by three tram, three bus and five Green Line routes (these too restarted in 1946) but the new Brighton Road had to make do with just one bus route. This was the 115, which took slightly under an hour to follow a highly roundabout route from Wallington to finish up not very far from where it had started, at Croydon Airport. Throughout the war it had been operated by STs, but changes

TON ROAD

Top: *A summer afternoon in June 1963, and London Transport Guy Special/ECW no.GS12 takes on passengers at Crawley bus station before leaving for Horsham on route 852.*
Michael Dryhurst

Above: *The influx of Leyland Tiger PS1s helped Southdown upgrade its coach fleet in the early postwar period. Now preserved is no.1303, a 1948 PS1/1 with Park Royal body.*
Michael H C Baker

The 1964 HCVC London-Brighton run was graced with three entries from the Museum of British Transport at Clapham, London. Two are seen here – 1920 London General K424 and, in the background, 1931 Green Line AEC Regal/Duple T219.
Michael Dryhurst

were afoot. Sutton garage, which provided half its allocation, was putting its new Daimler CWA6s on the route whilst later in the year Croydon, which provided the other half, would introduce all-Leyland PD1s. Shortly, of course, the all-conquering RT would supersede everything else. By quite a coincidence the coaches would have felt very much at home, for down on the Sussex coast Southdown was in the process of putting into service PD1s with Park Royal bodies identical to those fitted to London's Daimlers, whilst the new year would bring more PD1s with Leyland bodies.

I waited with eager anticipation outside the Victory garage by the pond for the Brighton coach and eventually it appeared, a Leyland Tiger TS7 with handsome Harrington body with a luggage compartment on the roof, which was somewhat superfluous for us day-trippers. Not that we were unencumbered for we always took comestibles with us – sandwiches wrapped in greaseproof paper, mother's homemade buns, and a thermos of tea with the milk in a former medicine bottle held firmly in place by a cork stopper and more greaseproof paper. Prewar Tigers monopolised the express services for the rest of 1946 but in the spring of 1947 in time for the summer season the first of a large fleet of PS1s began to arrive. These were not so much replacements for existing coaches, rather for the many which had been taken over for military service and never returned. Indeed many of the prewar Tigers had scarcely begun their careers for they were to serve

as front-line vehicles until the late 1950s. Southdown set the highest standards and it says much for the company, Leyland and, above all, the bodybuilders, that these vehicles were still perfectly acceptable to the travelling public after 20 years' service.

The first PS1s were put to work, not surprisingly, on the Brighton run, this being the company's most prestigious service. They were quite unlike anything else Southdown had owned for they were fitted with ECW bodywork. Although basically similar to ECW's standard bus body, they had many modifications, inside and out, and, painted in standard Southdown livery, they did not look in the least out of place. They were later downgraded to buses but served the company well, and one even lasted long enough (albeit as a left-luggage office) for me to photograph it alongside one of the first Leyland Nationals at Bognor Regis in 1973.

Superior

How superior we felt in our luxurious coach as we glided along Thornton Road, dipping under the trolleybus wires where we crossed the 630s on their way to 'near Willesden Junction' (wherever that was,

Representing Southdown in the area, a brand-new Queen Mary, Leyland Titan PD3/4 no.262 with Northern Counties bodywork, leaves the company's Central Works at Portslade for delivery to its operating garage in April 1965.
Michael Dryhurst

somewhere far away to the north-west), looked down on ordinary mortals waiting at bus stops for the 115 on Purley Way, held our noses as we passed Croydon Gas Works (when I asked why anyone should chose to live near such a nasty smell I was told it was good for their health – pull the other one), briefly encountered Country Area STLs, then under more trolleybus wires, this time the foreshortened 654s that had been specially designed to negotiate the precipitous Norwood Heights up to Crystal Palace. Earlier that year I'd been to my first Football League match there and seen the legendary Tommy Lawton who had just left Arsenal to become player manager of Notts County.

Next came Croydon Airport, in the process of being superseded as London's premier terminal as its runway could not safely accommodate the four-engined airliners then entering service, but it was still very busy with DC-3s, Dragon Rapides and the like. Over the hill and down to Purley to rejoin the old main road and a glimpse of a tram about to head back for the Embankment. Purley was the furthest south London trams ever reached; it's a moot point whether Croydon's new generation, the Tramlink system, actually penetrate further south at its New Addington terminus, there can only be few hundred yards in it either way.

Coulsdon saw the last of London's red buses but green 405s and 414s would keep us company as far as Redhill, the former continuing a good deal further down the A23 past Gatwick to Crawley. Gatwick Airport was a mere grass field in 1946 and the adjacent racecourse generated more business. The RT would begin to take over from the STL by 1950 and work the 405 and 414 for over 20 years – and even when London Country eventually phased them out they continued to make regular appearances, for there have often been more members of the RT family on the annual HCVS run than any other single type of PSV, whether as official entries or as accompanying vehicles.

Traffic

When we think of the enormous increase in traffic since prewar and immediate postwar days it is salutary to recall that the actual number of road traffic fatalities has declined. Cars were not only driven far less carefully, they and the roads were infinitely less well-designed in safety terms. So bad was the situation in the Crawley area that the hospital had to be enlarged in the 1930s to cope with motoring accidents. Southdown buses and coaches played virtually no part in this sad state of affairs – beautifully maintained and carefully driven by drivers who were proud to wear the Southdown uniform, they had an exemplary safety record,

It had not always been so. A horrendous accident on the Brighton road set back long-distance road travel by something like a decade when on 12 July

Left: *An unusual Brighton Hove & District bus, 1959 Bristol Lodekka LDS6B no.2, with a convertible open-top ECW body. The LDS Lodekka was the first flat-floor version of this model, and only eight production examples were built, all for BH&D. A normal radiator grille was felt to be unnecessary because of the Cave-Brown-Cave heating/ventilating system, but traditional grilles were soon added. The LDS models provided the foundation for the new F series Lodekka range.*
Michael Dryhurst

Below: *A later convertible open-topper, its passengers no doubt wishing it had a top cover. This Bristol Lodekka FS6G with ECW convertible open-top body was new in 1962 to Brighton Hove & District, and is seen after it passed into Southdown hands under NBC, in Kings Road, Brighton, in August 1977.*
Michael Dryhurst

1906 a Vanguard Milnes-Daimler double-decker on a day trip from London to Brighton suffered a transmission failure, ran out of control on Handcross Hill south of Crawley and ten passengers died. It was only after World War 1, when technology had moved on a great deal and surplus WD vehicles were cheaply available, that things got under way again. A rail strike in 1919 saw Southdown operating an emergency service between London and Brighton; regular express services began in 1924.

Southdown territory

At Crawley we were in Southdown bus territory proper, although London Transport had a garage here too. It was possible to travel all the way from Croydon to Brighton by double-deck service bus with just one change for LT's 405 met Southdown route 23 at Crawley. This latter ran to Brighton by way of Handcross, Cuckfield, Haywards Heath, Ditchling and Patcham. It took a fair while, but not a wildly

impractical one. If you caught the 09.33 from West Croydon it would get you into Crawley bus station at 10.59; you nipped smartly across to the waiting 23, which departed one minute later and deposited you at Pool Valley, Brighton, at 12.41. This was roughly an hour longer than the coach service from Thornton Heath Pond. The 405 ran at half-hourly intervals, the 23 every hour.

The coach station at Brighton was at Steine Street, a poky establishment – why was this the norm for coach stations? – but handy for the seafront. Bus services used Pool Valley, across the Steine Gardens and even nearer the sea; this was rather more spacious. Although handy for trippers and from an operating point of view, it was not particularly near many of the shops, especially in later years when the Churchill Square complex was opened in the 1960s and gradually bus services moved up there and Pool Valley is now the coach terminus, a handy and quite civilised arrangement.

Keeping score

Although Southdown was the recognised supplier of express coach services between London and Brighton, at weekends and holiday periods all manner of liveries, then as now, could be seen on the Brighton Road. A favourite pastime shared with my father was to stand beside the pond on a Sunday evening in August and watch the traffic heading back to London. To make it even more interesting, he would choose, say, Austin 7s and Grey-Green coaches, I would choose perhaps Morris 8s or Ford Prefects and Orange Luxury Coaches, and we would see who could get the highest totals. After an hour or so we would be up to cricket score proportions.

I might also note makes; Duple-bodied Bedford OBs would always win hands down. A little later when the first SBs with Vega bodywork appeared, they seemed to me quite enormous and luxurious by comparison, almost Transatlantic in their opulence. There were, of course plenty of Regals and Tigers; Timpsons favoured the former, Grey-Green the latter. I ought to remember what make Orange specialised in, for I knew its garage at Brixton well, but memory fails me although I have an idea that Bedfords figured in the fleet. There were a fair number of Dennises to be seen, the odd Daimler, Guy, Austin and Commer, but I don't recall Bristols on the A23, except for Brighton, Hove & District double-deckers being delivered, nor BMMOs, though Midland Red did sometimes work to Brighton. I expect a few wheezy old Tillings-Stevens were still to be seen in the early postwar period, but I doubt whether a foreigner of any description would be seen on the Brighton Road at this time.

And what about Brighton itself? Southdown, of course, with double- and single-deck buses serving every part of Sussex and across the borders to Kent (the 119 and 122 to Tunbridge Wells and Gravesend) and Hampshire (the famous 31 to Southsea). I've written at some length on this astonishingly popular company so perhaps this time the spotlight should focus on the two other concerns that served Brighton and its suburbs. These were the Corporation and the

Ideal trolleybus terrain – the steep Braybon Avenue in Brighton. But trolleybuses served the town for only 22 years, and shortly before the final conversion in June 1961, two vehicles from the original Brighton fleet pass. Both are AEC 661Ts with Weymann bodies.
Michael Dryhurst

Tilling company, Brighton, Hove & District. I shall get into fearful trouble for even implying that Hove is a mere suburb of Brighton, but I hope the fact that this select resort was given equal billing in the company title with its neighbour will allay any such suspicions.

Archaic

Being a Tilling company, Brighton, Hove & District operated buses in the 1930s which were identical to those which worked out of its London garages, hence their LT codes, TC (Tilling Croydon), TB (Tilling Bromley) and TL (Tilling Lewisham – although it was actually Catford). These were AEC Regents, the ST class and the longer STL class. Both had Tilling's own somewhat archaic bodywork, the former with open

staircases. One of the London STs, ST922, is preserved in working order at Cobham. The first modern, open-top buses purpose-built for seaside service anywhere in the country, were put to work in Brighton in 1936, being 1930 chassis, lengthened and fitted with bodies built in the company's own workshops.

In later years being a Tilling company meant that it was inevitable that Bristols would appear in the BH&D fleet, and in the immediate postwar years these predominated, the first having arrived in 1936. A large amount of rebuilding and rebodying went on at this time, but from 1946 onwards the Bristol K type with ECW body became the norm as elsewhere in the Tilling empire, although Brighton always stipulated highbridge bodywork. However Brighton considered to assert its individuality and, seeing no need for the Lodekka, it remained faithful to the highbridge K type, becoming its very last customer, in the summer of 1957. The withdrawal of all other types meant that by March 1959 it operated nothing but Ks. Four of these provided an echo of former

practice for they were ex-London buses, utility K6As dating from 1946, bought by Brighton in 1953 and rebodied by ECW in 1955.

Lodekkas

However Bristol Lodekkas eventually arrived, in April 1959. Thus, when Southdown absorbed Brighton, Hove & District in 1969, Lodekkas formed the bulk of the fleet. The last Ks, none of which ever received National livery, finished passenger service on 30 October 1971. The Lodekkas began to emerge in Southdown green/cream around the same time, but this was only a temporary measure for the sombre NBC green replaced this a year later. It was perhaps ironic that the very last bus to retain the much more attractive apple green/primrose livery was not of Southdown origin at all but former BH&D rear-entrance FS Lodekka no.21, delivered in 1960.

With the break-up of the National Bus Company, Brighton, Hove & District was reborn as Brighton & Hove. The long-time favourite Bristol/ECW combination of the old Tilling days was much in evidence, although the livery was now predominantly cream, but with vestiges of the traditional red. A reminder of an earlier generation is no.6447 (HAP 985). This is an ECW-bodied K type that entered service in Brighton in 1953, was sold 16 years later, and was then re-purchased in 1986. It was restored in the company workshops to its original pristine condition and is a regular sight at rallies on the South Coast.

For 20 years the Brighton Corporation motorbus fleet was 100% AEC but it turned to Leyland for Titan PD2/37s from 1959. In 1961 newly-delivered no.13 with Weymann forward-entrance body, sits at Old Steine. Although it retains the red/cream livery, the fleetname changed to Brighton Corporation in place of Brighton Hove & District following the withdrawal of the trolleybuses. It will be noted that Brighton clearly believed in maximising advertising revenue from its fleet.
Gavin Booth

Trolleybuses

The other concern in Brighton was the Corporation. It had operated trams until 1939, in which year it had replaced them with 44 Weymann-bodied AEC 661T trolleybuses. A joint agreement with Brighton, Hove & District meant that the latter purchased eight identical trolleybuses. At the same time the Corporation bought 21 AEC Regents, also with Weymann bodies. Nos.60-9 had all-metal bodies and were extraordinarily long-lived; they served in unmodified form for between 25 and 27 years. Corporation livery was to all intents and purposes identical to that of BH&D; indeed, it was some time before I realised they were separate concerns. I always considered the Weymann body of the late 1930s and early postwar years particularly handsome, and, painted in the well-proportioned Brighton livery, with the long AEC radiator and always well maintained, there wasn't a finer-looking bus in the land. Fortunately Michael Dryhurst bought no.63 for preservation when it was withdrawn in May 1965.

Having owned it for 30 years he sold it to Messrs Pye and Nicholson who gave the bus a very thorough overhaul, including an extensive refurbishment of the engine. They showed me over no.63 on one of its recent visit to the Chalkpits Museum at Amberley. I've always thought the AEC Regent/Weymann combination of the late 1930s/early postwar era an all-time classic and in the dignified red/cream Brighton Corporation livery with its beautifully appointed interior no.63 is one of the finest examples of the bus builders art.

Brighton gave up on trolleybuses in 1961. All but one of the original batch ended their days in a scrapyard in an old quarry in the South Downs just outside Lewes, but the 12 postwar Weymann-bodied BUT batch (four of which were the property of Brighton, Hove & District) found new owners in Bournemouth, Bradford and Maidstone. One, no.52 (LCD 52), dating from 1951, is preserved in Maidstone Corporation livery at the East Anglian Transport Museum near Lowestoft.

In addition to Leyland Titan PD2s, Brighton Corporation surprised many when it bought four Titan TD5s from nearby Southdown in 1961 as part of its fleet to complete the trolleybus replacement. No.19, a 1938 TD5 with 1949 East Lancs body.
Gavin Booth

Guinea pig

Twenty PD2/37 Leyland Titans with Orion rear-entrance bodies replaced the first group of withdrawn trolleybuses, 16 forward-entrance MCW-bodied Titans being the choice for the final batch. These all lasted until the 1970s, the first to be withdrawn, rear-entrance no.52, being used as a guinea pig for a new livery in March 1970. It was the trolleybuses that had dictated a common livery for the two concerns but now these had gone the Corporation decided to go its own way and French light blue/white was decided upon. Apparently it represented the sea and cliffs; if so it was lost on me – I always considered it rather effete.

Rear engines arrived in 1971 in the shape of Willowbrook-bodied Atlanteans. The company became known as Brighton Blue Bus in May 1994, but this title lasted only three years for in 1997 it was bought by the Brighton & Hove Bus & Coach Company. This meant that the former Tilling company was now at last responsible for the vast majority of bus services in and around Brighton and Hove. Since then it has become one of the most enterprising operators in the country. A new livery of predominantly cream with diagonal stripes of various colours was adopted, and the fleet has undergone constant updating. Old favourites such as

Yes, it snows in Brighton. Corporation no.5, a 1961 Leyland Titan PD2/37 with forward entrance Weymann body, at Hollingbury in January 1963. Michael Dryhurst

the long-serving VRs ended their service in Brighton in the spring of 2000, followed by the Nationals a few months later. Love them or loathe them, some of these, with C-prefix registrations, were amongst the last Nationals built. One of the driving forces behind the concept of the Leyland National was that it would be exported in thousands. That this never happened helped bring the Leyland company to its knees, so it is ironic that a couple of the former Brighton examples have found a new home, about as far away from Britain as one can get, in the Falkland Islands. Their successors, the Lynxes, the last Leylands in the fleet, followed shortly; Dennis Darts have become firm favourites, but there are also many double-deckers, the oldest being East Lancs-bodied Scanias. Low-floor double-deckers arrived in 1999 in the shape of 20 Tridents, the first of a growing fleet. One of the many individual touches of the modern Brighton fleet is the naming of some of its vehicles after characters associated with the town. These vary from such contemporary celebrities as Des Lynam, Sally Gunnell and Sir Norman Wisdom to historical ones like the Prince Regent and Phoebe Hessel. Not a lot of people know that the last-named was a lady who served in the army as a man for 17 years in Napoleonic times and is buried in St Nicholas's churchyard in the town centre near Churchill Square, the main bus alighting and boarding point.

Cosmopolitan

Brighton and Hove together encompass some of the most cosmopolitan communities in the kingdom. Created a city at the beginning of the new millennium, Brighton has long been known as London by the Sea. All sorts of famous theatricals have lived, and continue to live there. Brighton and Hove probably possess the finest range of seaside architecture in the country, ranging from the quite extraordinary Royal Pavilion, through the magnificent terraces of the early 19th century, to the railway station, and the yet-to-be-restored West Pier, although we'd do well to ignore some more recent disasters such as the Marina. In the 1930s Brighton became notorious for the gangs associated with the racecourse, immortalised in Graham Greene's masterpiece *Brighton Rock*. And in the 19th century, Dickens and Kipling lived here. The establishment of Sussex University in the 1960s added yet another dimension to its population, whilst the present-day annual festival, including art exhibitions of a very high standard held all over the city and musical and theatrical events of every possible (and some almost impossible description), has something for everyone. Even the world's greatest radio comedy show, *I'm Sorry I Haven't a Clue*, has been broadcast from Brighton. In short it is a pretty tolerant, laid-back but vibrant sort of place where just about every lifestyle can be accommodated. It was – and to an certain

extent still is – the only industrial town on this part of the South Coast, and a significant proportion of its population has always found it hard to make ends meet.

Public transport is vital to a lot of people in the city, and the Brighton & Hove Bus and Coach Company has proved itself to be one of the most enterprising in the country. It now reaches far out beyond the original confines of the old borough, having inherited many of the long-distance routes once operated by Southdown. It is always ready to offer various travel concessions, and a flat fare of £1 for a single journey within the city, introduced experimentally in January 2001, has, not surprisingly, proved so successful that it remains in operation. As a consquence, besides having a fleet that is maintained in excellent condition, Brighton is one of the few places outside London where bus travel is on the increase. **CB**

Below: *Brighton Corporation decided to establish its own identity following the abandonment of the trolleybuses and a French light blue/white livery was decided upon. It is worn by no.85, a Leyland Atlantean/Willowbrook bought in 1971 – the first double-deckers for the undertaking bodied outside the MCW organisation.*
Michael Dryhurst

Born: 1904, when the Corporation took over three horse-tram routes developed by the Exeter Tramway Company since 1882. The Corporation electrified and extended the system between April 1905 and 1929, when the last new trams arrived.

How long did the trams last?:
An incredibly short time after the last four double-deckers arrived. Traffic congestion in the city was becoming a major problem and, as in many other parts of the country at the time, the received wisdom was that trams contributed to this. The last services came off on 19 August 1931 and the newest quartet was sold for further service in Halifax. The trams also were victims of advances in bus design.

Exeter had begun to embrace the bus?: Devon General was already operating in and from the city, but the Corporation followed in 1929, with three routes and three different types of single-deck bus.

And these were?: Two Leyland Lion PLSC3s, two Bristol Bs and three Maudslay ML3s. The Maudslays appear to have impressed most as six more arrived in 1930, while a 20-seat Commer Invader replaced a poorly maintained extremity of the tram system. The Commer didn't last long, and the hardware that killed off the trams was much bigger.

Exeter went double-deck?: Certainly did. Although Leyland exhorted the industry to buy one of its Titans and bury a tram, Exeter considered alternatives to the revolutionary TD1 from Lancashire. It borrowed a Daimler and two AECs and it was the latter than won its first order. Six Regents with Ransomes bodies arrived along with a single-deck Regal to replace the unloved Commer. Nine more Regents came in 1931 along with another Maudslay, but the Titan also found favour. Ten Brush-bodied TD1s replaced the last trams.

No.1:
Exeter Corporation Transport

How many routes were there?:
By 1933 the Corporation had a stable network of eight, all identified – as their Stagecoach successors remain identified today – by route letters rather than numbers.

What about the fleet?: The next big advance was to start going over to diesels from 1934, when three double-deck demonstrators – a Regent, a Titan and a Bristol GO5G – were borrowed and later purchased. Surprisingly, another four Bristols followed them in 1935, but subsequent prewar purchases were of Leyland Titans and Tigers with a mix of Cravens and Leyland bodywork. They were followed by utility Bedford OWB single-deckers and Daimler CWA6 and CWD6 double-deckers. Postwar purchasing was a mix of wartime and prewar practice, with 17 Leyland PD2s and 30 Daimler CVD6 double and single-deckers. Guy Arab IVs became a surprise new favourite during the 1950s, before Exeter took to the Leyland PD2 again, mainly with Massey bodywork. It also got 10 Leyland Leopards and Panthers.

How did it get on with its neighbours?: The Corporation struck an agreement with Devon General in 1947, each operating half of the mileage of services within 10 miles of the city centre. As a result, Corporation buses ran out to places like Exmouth and Budleigh Salterton, while Devon General ran some of the city routes. But the Corporation had problems.

Like?: Losing money. By 1969 the transport department was reckoned to be losing £25,000 a year and the Corporation was open to an offer from the National Bus Company, which by then owned Devon General and was about to amalgamate it with Western National. On 1 April 1970 Devon General paid £190,000 for Exeter's 65 buses and its former tram depot, which survived until a new one opened in 1973. It also inherited an order for seven more Panthers.

And what happened to the livery?:
For a time, NBC kept the green-and-cream livery, with the word 'Exeter' replacing 'City of Exeter' or 'Exeter Corporation', but most buses soon went into poppy red with Devon General fleetnames. An Arab IV was kept in Exeter green as a gesture to tradition, although the bus itself wandered far beyond its home city. Green became one of the route colours adopted by the privatised Devon General, when then owner Harry Blundred did exciting things with urban minibuses in the 1980s and early 1990s.

Alan Millar

Traditional fare for Exeter Corporation – a 1948 Leyland Titan PD2/1 with Leyland bodywork featuring an interesting mix of sliding and half-drop windows.
Gavin Booth

THREE IN A ROW

CHRIS DREW's first selection of triple-number registrations

September 1 2001 is not a date that will be found often inside the covers of *Classic Bus*, but it marked a very important day the annals of vehicle registration. With the introduction of the new British vehicle registration system the idea of matching registration numbers and fleetnumbers simply flew out the window. This got me to thinking of some of the triple-number registrations that won't appear again in my lifetime. The cross-section of time chosen was dictated by the collection of Ian Allan 'British Bus Fleets' books I bought in the mid-1960s. The books covered the vehicles that had worked for the previous 20-25 years.

More of my drawings of triple-number-registered buses can be found on pages 31, 73, 100 and 120.

000

OK, it's not a number itself, but add a single digit at the front and a couple of letters and Bob's your uncle. There weren't that many to choose from, but some of what there were were important. Two prototypes, both Daimlers, take pride of place: 6000 EH, the Roadliner which was shown at the 1964 Commercial Motor Show in the colours of PMT, and 7000 HP the sadly-missed Fleetline which was destroyed by fire whilst in the ownership of Blue Bus Services, Willington. There were a brace of AEC Reliances – 9000 WB, a Roe-bodied version from Sheffield (see page 122), and FT 9000 with Weymann Fanfare bodywork in the care of Wakefields, part of the Northern General group at the time. I chose 6000 EH as a representative.

111

The task became easier from this point on, although, considering the number of buses registered in the time frame chosen, there was not a large selection here. The list comprised an open-top Leyland PD1 from Eastbourne, Regent Vs from Bradford and Liverpool, Royal Tigers from Cumberland and Manchester (the Manchester examples being rear-loaders, just to add interest), Fleetlines from Middlesbrough and Sheffield, a Crossley from Luton and another bus from Cumberland, this time a Bristol FS. From north of the border came a yellow-cloaked Albion Lowlander from Alexander Northern and (in the drawing) a Bedford SB for Mitchell's of Stornoway, of whom more later.

THE GAME C

Names for types of bus and coach are usually easier to remember than numbers, says GAVIN BOOTH – with the emphasis on 'usually'

PRIVATE

XRW 401

THE ONLY TIME I was involved in naming a range of buses was when I was doing public relations work for Walter Alexander, and names were required for a new body being developed for the Dennis Dart and Volvo B6 midibus chassis that were beginning to catch on in the early 1990s. Alexander hadn't used names before, but we had all got used to the letters it used, most famously the Y type single-decker; new management decided that names might be more memorable, so I pored through dictionaries and we brainstormed names, carefully watching lists we had obtained showing names that were already in use by vehicle manufacturers, or were reserved for future use.

The eventual choice was 'Dash', a partial nod to the Dennis Dart, which was selling well by the time – although the first Dash was mounted on the new Volvo B6 chassis. The Dash was followed by the Strider for full-size single-deckers – a definite nod to Yorkshire Rider, the target customer – and the

Above: Daimler's first foray into chassis type names was the Freeline, a heavyweight underfloor-engined model. In 1959 Coventry Corporation received three of these Freelines with Willowbrook Viking bodies.
All photos by Gavin Booth

Above right: Guy used the Arab name for single-deck and double-deck models for some 35 years, the best-remembered being the wartime and postwar Arab double-deckers. Although the Arab I and Arab II designations were unofficial ones applied by enthusiasts, Guy later adopted this numbering series for MkIII, MkIV and MkV Arabs. These Arab IVs sitting in the Hawkhead yard of Graham's of Paisley include a number of former East Kent examples with Park Royal bodies.

Right: Leyland stuck mainly to animal names for its single-deckers. This former Northern General Tiger Cub of Paton of Renfrew has attractive Saro bodywork, built by Saunders-Roe. Although Saro is sometimes used as the company name, it is thought to be a name applied to certain styles of body – though, confusingly, there were double-deck Saro bodies too.

Above: *Coachbuilders had named their bodies from an early stage, and by the 1960s were adopting names that suggested strength – as with the Duple Commander, here. Duple would later produce the Dominant, while arch-rival Plaxton went for the Paramount. This is a Commander 36, referring to the length in feet, built by Duple (Northern) – formerly Burlingham – at Blackpool. It is seen at Earls Court in 1966, ready to take its place on the Duple stand, the windscreen sticker suggesting that the bodywork costs £4,375. The chassis is the Leyland Leopard, continuing the animal theme.*

Left: *Some manufacturers returned to names they had previously used. AEC's first Reliance was a 1928 model, but the best-remembered Reliance is the 1953-introduced underfloor-engined model that remained in production for more than 25 years. The Reliance name broke away from AEC's line of Regal single-deckers, and although the chassis specification changed over the period, it was always called the Reliance; Leyland was more likely to find new names for variations on the same theme. This Reliance, seen in Edinburgh, was in the fleet of the Scottish Co-operative Wholesale Society, Glasgow, whose coaches went under the Majestic name. The bodywork, by Alexander, is the Y type – just a designation in an alphabetical series, but possibly one of the best-known of its time.*

minibus body became the Sprint. The only other name that was adopted at the time was Royale, given to the R type double-deck body with a more rounded front and square-edged side glazing.

Royale apart, Alexander's Dash/Strider/Sprint range had an obvious common theme, and looking at how manufacturers have chosen to name their vehicles – if indeed they choose to – it is interesting to identify those themes and also wonder what on earth they were thinking when some names were selected.

Goods models

Early buses were identified by letters or numbers or both. Many were derived from goods models, and

there was no incentive to distinguish models by name. It was only when 'real' bus chassis came along, with lower-built chassis designed for passenger access, that manufacturers started to allocate names.

It's always dangerous to make a claim for the first time anything happened in the bus world. There are thousands of experts out there ready to dispute any 'fact'. But it does seem likely that the first names were applied to models in the 1920s, when manufacturers were starting to develop lower-slung chassis designed specifically for bus operation. As a Scot I would love to think that Albion started the trend, and it seems that maybe it happened that way. Its Model 24, introduced at the 1923 Olympia Show,

Also owned by SCWS, Glasgow, the bus fleet trading as Smith's of Barrhead. The last four double-deckers bought for the fleet were lowheight AECs, two Bridgemasters and two Renowns. At the Paisley Abbey terminus the two 1961 Bridgemasters are passed by one of the 1963 Renowns. Bridgemaster was a clever name for a lowheight double-decker, doubtless influenced by the Routemaster, while Renown returned to a name it first used in 1929.

seems to have been named Viking – a name that Albion would return to at regular intervals for the rest of its existence. Albion went for a 'V' theme – Victor, Valiant, Valkyrie, Valorous and Venturer – but after acquisition by Leyland the names were rather more descriptive of the model, hence the midi-size Nimbus in 1955, the thrifty Aberdonian in 1957 and the lowheight Lowlander in 1961.

If Albion wasn't the very first, it was certainly one of the first. Leyland had relied on letter codes for its models, but from 1925 turned to names, supported by letter/number codes that said a bit more about the exact specification. The 1925 L range of chassis introduced names to the company's list – Leviathan, Leveret, Lioness, Leopard and Lion; the last two would be names associated with Leyland almost to the end of its existence.

AEC also used names from 1925 – Renown, Blenheim, Ramillies and Grenville, on a Royal Navy theme – and returned in 1929 with names that would become much more familiar to later generations.

Me-too

You suspect there was a bit of 'me too' about naming chassis in the 1920s. Other manufacturers who scoured the dictionaries for new names – with varying degrees of success, it must be said – included Thornycroft (Boadicea, Speedy, Ardent, Cygnet, Daring), Sunbeam (Sikh, Pathan), AJS (Pilot, Commodore, Admiral), Tilling-Stevens (Express), Crossley (Eagle, Hawk, Alpha), Commer (Avenger)

and Karrier (which went for a 'C' theme with Clipper, Consort, Coaster, Cutter and Chaser Six).

If some of these names are unfamiliar, it is because the models, and sometimes the manufacturers, didn't enjoy great successs. Certainly not when compared with the emerging giants – AEC and Leyland.

Leyland's next move from its 1925 L range was the 1927 T range based on the new six-cylinder T type engine. The single-decker was the Tiger, the main double-decker the Titan and the three-axle double-decker the Titanic – this only 15 years after the eponymous liner sank in the Atlantic. The Tiger and Titan names would continue to be used for more than 50 years.

AEC's 1929 equivalents were the single-deck Regal, double-deck Regent and three-axle Renown. The R theme had been established in 1928 with the interim six-cylinder Reliance chassis, but like the other 'R' names, the Reliance would have a long and distinguished history in postwar years as the company's main underfloor-engined single-deck offering.

Top: *AEC stuck with the Regent name from 1929 right to the end of double-deck production at AEC in 1968. This is a Newcastle Corporation Regent V of 1957 with attractive Park Royal bodywork, in Northumberland Street, Newcastle.*

Above: *Leyland made no bones about its ambitions with the Royal Tiger Worldmaster, a rugged and powerful chassis that won business from all around the world. CIÉ bought 23 Worldmasters in 1962 with this style of Ogle-designed bodywork, and these were followed by 13 similarly-bodied Leopards, to suit contemporary PSV regulations in Northern Ireland. ET3, one of the Leopards, toured the UK in 1964 promoting Irish tourism, and it is seen in Princes Street station, Edinburgh.*

Left: *Although the classic London Transport RT type is a variant of AEC's Regent III, it is probably most often referred to as simply an RT – though quite what these letters stand for has long been a subject of controversy in the pages of* Classic Bus. *RT4009 simmers in the sun at Laleham in 1970 before setting off on its short journey to Staines.*

Below: *Probably the best name of all, and one that is widely recognised by the general public – even though it tends to be applied to any halfcab double-decker – is the Routemaster, an inspired choice by London Transport. On early examples the name was applied above the fleetnumber, rather as LGOC had done with its London Six type a quarter of a century earlier. RM367, in original condition, sits at Hammersmith in 1960.*

Steadfast, Nippy and, my particular favourite, the Beautyride. Maudslay went for alliteration, so we had the Marathon, Magna, Montrose, Masta, Meteor and Mentor. So did Commer with the Centaur, Corinthian and Centurion. Guy had started with the Runabout and Premier Six in the 1920s and in the 1930s turned to Victory (a name it would return to) and Conquest, and, like Leyland, it went for an animal theme, but only for its smaller models, giving us the Wolf, Vixen and Otter. Guy's best-remembered model name, the Arab, first appeared in 1933.

Themes

Already, themes are appearing. The alphabetical approach obviously appealed to some manufacturers, and while AEC stuck with its R theme through the 1930s, and re-used these names, it clearly decided in the 1950s that the name should have more to do with the model. Leyland, on the other hand, had already set a pattern where single-deckers would normally be named after animals, the famous Leyland Zoo, and double-deckers after mythological creatures. So Leyland's other 1930s single-deckers were the Cub, Cheetah, Badger, Gnu and Panda.

Thornycroft was not so precise in its names, so in the 1930s we got the Lightning, Handy, Dainty,

Crossley chose Condor for its 1930 double-deck model, but its 1934 development was the Mancunian, a nod to the location of its works and its prime target customer. Morris Commercial went for important titles – Viceroy, Imperial, Director and (maybe not such a good idea in the 1930s) Dictator.

Dennis, still building in Guildford today, used names that would become familiar again in recent times – Dart, Arrow, Falcon, Lance and Lancet; its 'sharp things' theme continues to this day with chassis like the Javelin and Trident.

Leyland gave the name Aberdonian to its thrifty lightweight Tiger Cub. This is a former Northern General MR11N Aberdonian with Weymann body, operating with Golden Miller at Shepperton station in 1970.

Missing

Some well-known makes are missing from the article so far, because they only used letters and numbers. Bristol and Daimler, for instance, had not dissimilar codes that told you a bit about the chassis. So the main 1930s Bristol types were the K and L, typically K5G and L5G telling us they had 5LW Gardner engines; Daimler's main range from the mid-1930s was the CO series (commercial oil-engined) and the most popular variant was the COG5 with the Gardner 5LW. Bedford used letters, only breaking that pattern in its later life with the Venturer.

And what about trolleybuses, you ask. Again I am prepared to be proved wrong, but it doesn't look as if any manufacturer named a trolleybus chassis. Even AEC and Leyland, which had used names for its motorbuses from the mid-1920s, stuck to letter/number codes, even during the height of the 1930s trolleybus-buying boom.

After World War 2, manufacturers were working on new types of chassis, which merited a new set of names.

The underfloor-engined single-decker was all the rage in the early 1950s, and manufacturers dreamt up new names – and in some cases used or adapted old ones. So AEC's first offering was the relatively unimaginative Regal IV, followed by the lightweight Reliance chassis and integrally-constructed Monocoach (a bus, in spite of the name); Daimler

broke the habit of a lifetime and called its underfloor single-decker the Freeline; Guy was more traditional and launched the Arab UF; Leyland started with the integral Olympic, followed by the Royal Tiger and lightweight Tiger Cub.

As the demand grew for more powerful single-deckers and, after legislation changed, longer ones, AEC stuck with Reliance, Leyland produced the Royal Tiger Worldmaster (mainly for export) and the short-run Royal Tiger Cub before settling on the Leopard as its main model.

Two newcomers to the bus business, Atkinson and Seddon, used names but, having found one, tended to stick to it. So Atkinson buses were usually Alphas and Seddons were Pennines. Seddon came up with a good name in 1972 for its small bus – Midi, a name that passed into regular generic use some 20 years later.

Lowheight

The next technical development was the lowheight double-decker, with a drop-centre rear axle allowing normal seating on both decks. The first and probably

the best was the first Bristol model graced by a name – the Lodekka. It would be Bristol's only named model; even its popular rear-engined single-decker was simply the RE, and its vertical-rear-engined double-decker the VR. AEC followed with the Bridgemaster, a slight nod to the Routemaster, in which it was heavily involved with London Transport, and later the Renown. Dennis built the Lodekka under licence as the Loline, and when Leyland finally got its act together, its offering was the Lowlander, typically badged as an Albion.

Leyland made the running with the move to rear-engined double-deckers. Its first was the Atlantean in 1956, followed by the Titan and finally by the Olympian. The Atlantean prototypes had been known as Lowloaders. Daimler's 1960 rear-engined model was the Fleetline, later built at Leyland and sold under the Leyland name. Dennis came into the market later with the Dominator, as did MCW with the Metrobus. Guy didn't produce a rear-engined double-decker; instead it developed an advanced front-engined model, the Wulfrunian, named after natives of the company's home town, Wolverhampton.

Rear-engined single-deckers followed. The AEC Swift and Merlin were variations of the same theme, as was Leyland's Panther, which spawned the shorter and lighter Panther Cub; Daimler chose the Roadliner name. But these chassis were swept away

Bristol's only named model was a good one – the Lodekka. These two Southdown Lodekkas are from the batch of eight unique LDS6B models supplied to Brighton, Hove & District in 1959. Three were convertible open-toppers like no.2001 on the left. A photo of one of these buses in original condition accompanies the Brighton Road article in this book.

under Leyland when the Leyland National appeared – the move away from animal names reflecting the joint company set up with National Bus Company.

Of the model names in use today, Dennis (now TransBus Guildford) uses the long-established Dart, the more recent Javelin and the much more recent Trident, but TransBus is moving to a range that mixes a name, in this case Enviro, with numbers that indicate the size of the model, rather in the style of Alexander's ALX range. So far we have the Enviro 300 (full-size single-decker) and Enviro 500 (three-axle double-decker) and there are more to come.

Citybus

Volvo has no real history of type names. It relented for the UK market with the Citybus, the underfloor-engined double-decker based on its market-leading B10M platform, and decided wisely to retain the Olympian name for the reworked chassis inherited from Leyland.

WATERLOO STN & 503 VICTORIA STN via Westminster Bridge

6 PAY AS YOU ENTER 6

JLA58D

Left: At least with Leyland you knew where you were – a Tiger was a single-decker (unless maybe it was a Cub, Lion or Cheetah) and a Titan was a double-decker (unless it was a Titanic or an Atlantean or . . .). These preserved Wigan buses are a 1932 Santus-bodied Tiger TS4 and a 1940 all-Leyland Titan TD7.

Above: *To AEC it was the Swift, to London Transport the Merlin, and to operators it was often a bit of a disaster. The first of London's famous 1966 Red Arrows had Strachans bodies, as here in Waterloo Road. Now Red Arrow – that's a good name.*

Optare introduced names that have come to describe the whole vehicle, even when these are body-on-chassis types like the Delta, Prisma, Vecta and Spectra. And it has its range of complete vehicles – MetroRider, Excel and Solo (so-low, a rare punning name); the MetroRider had been inherited when MCW pulled out of bus manufacture. In its years as a manufacturer of complete vehicles, MCW had also used the Metro prefix for the Metrobus and Metroliner.

The names given by bodybuilders to their products are worth an article on their own, but it was the builders of coach bodies that tended to make the running, often applying a bewilderingly large range of names to a small range of bodies. Duple got things started with the Vista in the 1930s, and for the next 40 years the 'V' names were usually applied to Bedford (alias Vauxhall) products. Plaxton only got into names in the 1950s, but its best-remembered names are probably the 1958 Panorama and 1982

Paramount – and although the 'P' theme was not used in the early days, in recent years it has become familiar, notably on the Premiere coach and Pointer midibus bodies – though the Pointer name was actually inherited from Reeve Burgess when that company was taken over.

Reincarnation

Bus bodybuilders only really came on stream with model names in the 1950s (MCW Orion, Hermes) but more recently we have seen East Lancs working hard to get the letter 'y' into its names (Lolyne, Cityzen, Pyoneer, Myllennium, Spryte, Flyte and Vyking). The Lolyne is almost a reincarnation of the 1950s Dennis chassis name and another current body is the Lowlander, reprising the Leyland-Albion name of the 1960s.

The current prize probably goes to the bus bodybuilder Wright, which seems to delight in naming its bodies, resulting in the Axcess Floline, for instance, the Solar Fusion or the Eclipse Gemini. When you understand the Wright system, you can (just) see the logic. But it's still confusing to remember that outwardly similar Wright single-deck bodies change their names depending on what chassis they are mounted on – so a Liberator (Volvo B10L) looks awfully like an Axcess-ultralow (Scania L113) or a Renown (Volvo B10BLE).

It was a lot easier when every Leyland double-decker was a Titan. **CB**

THE BRISTOL RE has become an icon. It's almost been sanctified in some quarters. For this was the one rear-engined single-decker of its generation – the 1960s – that seemed to work while its rivals all crumpled in a heap practically from the day they were born.

Like all icons and saints, it wasn't as perfect as legend would have it. In his recent exhaustive book on the breed, Duncan Roberts – an RE fan without doubt – also lifts the lid on its weaknesses, but that only puts the bus into a fairer perspective. It was still by far the best of its generation.

I have little doubt that other factors make it such a wonderbus among contemporary blunderbuses like the Swift, Panther, Roadliner, Panther Cub, single-deck Fleetline and Seddon RU. One was what one might call the Kennedy factor: like the American president in Dallas in 1963, it was slain prematurely before old age would show up its weaknesses and indiscretions. The other was that it sounded fantastic. An RE in deep, tuneful roar might not cut much ice with engineers, but it earned it a special place in the hearts of enthusiasts.

And while we're on the subject, I'll readily confess to being able – almost – to summon a memory in my mind's ears of those moments on overnight London-Glasgow journeys when a Western Scottish REMH coach would end many miles of top gear cruising and click into a whining low gear to negotiate a roundabout or climb a gradient. We're talking music here, a sound you may still have a few more months to snatch on a kerbside in Belfast before Citybus's last RELLs finally head off into history.

The truly impressive thing about the RE, though, is that Bristol got so much of it right from the start and that this bus was developed before Daimler and Leyland, as the Irish would put it so graphically, made such a hames of their counterpart products.

Prototypes

The prototypes appeared in 1962, around the same time as Daimler unveiled its first Roadliner and two years ahead of the AEC Swift and Leyland Panther. At the time, Bristol could sell its products only to other state-owned operators, so there was no great commercial pressure to produce the trendiest bus on our roads. Yet, here was the manufacturer responsible for the country's first successful lowheight double-decker – the Lodekka – developing the first successful rear-engined single-decker.

The umbilical cord that linked Bristol, Eastern Coach Works and the former Tilling operating

CLASSIC WONDERBUS

ALAN MILLAR
nominates the Bristol RE

The bus that started it all, Bristol RELL6G prototype 7431 HN with uniquely-fronted ECW body. It first entered service with United Auto as BR1 in December 1962.
G Coxon

Seen on the Isle of Anglesey is Crosville no.SRG117, a 1969 Bristol RELL6G with the deep-screen version of the Eastern Coach Works body most readily associated with this chassis.
Michael Dryhurst

companies allowed the manufacturer's engineers to develop its buses with lots of input from real operators who understood the reality of ensuring that their services ran as efficiently and reliably as possible. And they were able to eliminate the compromises that occur when working with a great range of independent bodybuilders.

The RE was designed from the outset to take advantage of the new 36ft length limit and, as Duncan Roberts's book reminds us, to replace life-expired, horribly awkward lowbridge double-deckers. The engine went at the back to keep the floor as low as possible, but as Tilling drivers were well schooled in the art of double-declutching, Bristol saw no need to fit anything other than a synchromesh gearbox in 1962.

Leyland could have done the same then, but its three-year-old mid-engined Leopard had bags of spare power in its original 30ft form, so it made sense then to stretch it to 36ft and look at rear engines later. Likewise, the AEC Reliance got itself more length and, ultimately, more power. On the other hand, Bristol could presumably have taken the same tack and stretched and upped the power of its mid-engined MW. Wisely, it didn't, and we've probably got the input of operators to thank for that.

Things looked up for the RE from 1965, when Leyland bought into Bristol and took its products into the open market. The Leyland connection added the option – soon the standard feature – of a semi-automatic gearbox, and the option of a Leyland engine. There also was an AEC engine option but, although Ulsterbus apparently came quite close to

ordering some, this particular possibility remained only on the pages of the company's catalogues.

Open-market availability took the RE into places Bristol could not have gone before, at a time when the industry thought it would largely desert the double-decker in pursuit of one-person operation. It's worth speculating today whether that movement would have progressed more smoothly had all of that first generation of rear-engined single-deckers been as good as the RE, for the likes of Hartlepool, South Shields and Warrington kept theirs for normal lifespans while others disposed of their AECs, Leylands and Daimlers.

Demand was so high by 1970 that Crosville, against the superior judgment of people who were going to have to operate the beasts, was prevailed upon to buy 100 Seddons because the RE was in short supply.

Marginalised

So why was it marginalised and all but killed off by 1974? The Leyland National, that's why. Now you can perceive some sort of devil incarnate in the people who took that decision and regard it as spite to snuff out all things Bristol.

I'm not sure that I buy into that idea, but the simple fact was that Leyland – again with input from

the same bus operators who helped fashion the RE – had gone into mass production with a new-generation integral single-decker intended for the home and export markets. This was exactly the same sort of product as the likes of Mercedes-Benz were building in Germany with similar export markets in mind. But Mercedes was a lot more successful in hitting its target markets than Leyland was with the National. So Leyland wasn't going to undermine itself by offering what it saw as duplicate products.

Few would have wept when the Panther, Swift and single-deck Fleetline joined the Roadliner in the land called oblivion. But the RE was a better bus and people tried to resist its demise. Leyland could probably have appeased most of them by offering the RE's Gardner 6HLX and Leyland 680 in place of the truly dreadful fixedhead 510, and eventually it was persuaded to do just that.

But it kept the RE alive mainly for two 'export' markets, one of which merited the description a lot more objectively than the other. These were markets that wanted a separate chassis and body, not least because there were understandable political reasons for specifying locally assembled bodywork. So the RE was kept going for New Zealand and for Northern Ireland.

Foreign

The mainland British public might often have wished that Ulster was a foreign land in the 1970s, but it was and still is part of the UK. Ulsterbus, however, was a powerful buyer run by a powerful managing director in German-born Werner Heubeck. It didn't want the complexity of the National and it provided most of the work for Alexander's Belfast factory. So a case was made for the RE to be kept in production for Ulsterbus and Citybus right up to the

Another Crosville RE, no.CRL260, an RELH6L (Leyland engine) with ECW's attractive coach body, in London in 1972. Michael Dryhurst

early 1980s when, finally, new legislation put paid to the 20-year-old design.

Rather than go integral then, Ulsterbus switched to mid engines and higher floors, and kept its body business with Alexander (Belfast).

Not that the RE itself was finished. Along with the National – whose indestructible body shell made up for the weakness of its engine – it became one of the buses of choice for operators taking advantage of the early years of deregulation from 1986. Good numbers of ECW-bodied examples were still available on the secondhand market and, thanks to the bodies' aluminium construction, they were a lot less badly affected by structural weakness or corrosion than others were. They had low enough floors for urban operation and they were relatively simple and cheap to maintain.

This new lease of life found them in a few surprising fleets, like Busways (the former Tyne & Wear PTE bus division) and Milton Keynes Citybus, while Hartlepool kept its fleet going right through its last lean years of council and employee ownership before Stagecoach moved in and modernised.

Ultimately, like all good machines and just like the last Ulsterbus and Citybus examples, time has ravaged REs beyond the point of sensible, economic repair, but that doesn't take away what they have achieved: a lifespan from launch to withdrawal of over 30 years, with individual lifespans well in excess of 20 years. They worked where others failed – and they sounded terrific. Yes, this was a wonderbus. **CB**

THREE IN A ROW

More CHRIS DREW drawings

222

I made a conscious decision not to enter London Transport into the reckoning because a fleet that size was bound to throw triples more often. Saying that, I was going to enter them from the secondhand market, which is how Grimsby's STL, and Dundee's Cravens-bodied RT found their way here. Maidstone & District produced a Bristol K, Leicester a Bridgemaster and Bury a PD3. A couple of odd Royal Tigers roared from the pages, a rear-entrance example from Sheffield and Lydney-covered one from Red & White. A trolleybus appeared in the guise of a BUT 9641T from Huddersfield, and from Newcastle one of its large fleet of Alexander-bodied Atlanteans. Northampton supplied its staple fare in the shape of a Roe-bodied Daimler CV (in drawing). Scotland's capital provided a Duple Bella Vista-bodied Bedford VAS and finally, DJS 222, a Duple-bodied Bedford SB for Mitchell's of Stornoway – and that's not the end of it!

333

A few rarities and oddments turned up here: a Roberts-bodied Foden single-decker from Alexander Northern, Glasgow D528, one of a batch of single-deck Daimler CVs with the Corporation's own bodywork, a Beadle-bodied AEC Reliance for East Kent and an all-Leyland PD2 for Barton – one of a few new ones, I believe. Portsmouth provided a Cravens-bodied trolley, while Hull and Sheffield supplied Regents, the former a III, the latter a V. A classic Burlingham Seagull came from Premier Travel and a first-generation Atlantean from Western Welsh (in picture). Just before I sign off, may I add JJS 333, a Bedford SB for, yes, Mitchell's.

WORTHY
WE ARE NOT

GAVIN BOOTH pays reluctant homage to the Routemaster as an introduction to GEOFF RIXON's colour pictures on the next eight pages

WE ALL THOUGHT that nothing would ever match the RT for longevity. Introduced by London Transport in 1939 and last operated by LT in 1979, it seemed unlikely that any other bus would equal or even beat that record.

Not for the first time we were wrong – oh so wrong. And not for the first time was I wrong about the bus that would break that record, the much-revered Routemaster. Those of us living beyond Watford got just a little sick of the Routemaster in the 1950s. London Transport was trumpeting its 'Bus of the Future', yet to my teenage eyes it seemed positively old-fashioned when you compared it with the exciting shape-of-things-to-come that was the Leyland Atlantean. The Routemaster was front-engined – how 1940s. It had an open rear platform – how non-U. It wasn't even 30ft long – how infra-dig. But that was youth and distance talking. There is a tendency when you are young to rail against what everybody else is saying. So the more my London friends raved about this amazing new bus that was entering service in impressive quantities, the more I countered with taunts about its 'dated' appearance.

OK, I was wrong. A few family trips to stay with relatives in the Harrow area gave me a chance to sample newly-introduced RMs on trolleybus replacement services in North London and, yes, they were all right. More than that they were good. No – more than that – they were very good. And now every time I am in London I find it impossible to resist contriving a trip on a Routemaster, or simply stand in Oxford Street and marvel at the sheer number still in service 49 years after the prototype was first shown, and 44 years since the first production examples entered service.

The fact that RMs came north to Scotland in the 1980s as competition-busters in the early days of deregulation may also have coloured my judgement. Here the Routemaster was out of the environment for which it was designed, and it was a delight to see how comfortably it dealt with routes like Clydeside's Glasgow-Paisley corridor or Kelvin's long 'tram route' from Easterhouse to Old Kilpatrick. Drivers, particularly those who didn't really like contact with passengers anyway, loved them, passengers loved having a conductor to chat with, and the bus companies loved them because they were so fast and manoeuvrable. And cheap.

Perhaps the problem back in the 1950s was the look of them. Cover up the slightly quirky bonnet, and the body was not a million miles from the RT. RM1's original front, almost flush with the front end, and reflecting the fact that the radiator was under the floor, was pretty but seemed to lack purpose. The next fronts for the prototype RMs looked like (and presumably were) afterthoughts grafted on to accommodate the radiator, which was now moved to the front. To my mind it was only when the front that was first seen at the 1958 Commercial Show on RM8 appeared that the Routemaster looked like a purposeful and modern piece of street furniture. That front end has been modified too – notably (and probably least successfully) with twin headlamps for the RMC and RCL coaches, but the very original version, with no AEC vee on the grille, and the registration plate as part of the grille, arguably still beats the rest.

The remaining 600+ Routemasters in London are rather less standardised than they were 35 years ago. Now you won't find one with a Leyland engine, will find few if any with AEC engines, and internally many have been refurbished at various stages, most recently by Marshalls, which undertook a programme of rebuilding former examples that had been bought back; the Marshall rebuilds have Cummins engines and Allison gearboxes.

Mayor Ken Livingstone repatriated these RMs because he is a fan of the type and of conductors, but the age of the remaining Routemaster fleet and changing legislation may bring about something that in recent years had seemed increasingly unlikely – the final demise of the type.

And what a day that will be! The RT received a well-deserved send-off in April 1979, but it is likely to pale into insignificance when the last Routemaster trundles into its garage. But before that there are the RM50 celebrations in 2004 when even old cynics like me will reluctantly agree that it was a pretty good bus.

For the moment, though, enjoy Geoff Rixon's colour shots. Not just red ones, I said to him, and he obliged. **CB**

Above: The Routemaster as many like to remember it – in London Transport livery with underlined fleetname and the original style of radiator grille. This is RM1610 of Cricklewood garage on route 16 in the Edgware Road in May 1967 fresh from its first overhaul. Use of the offside route-number box has already been abandoned – indeed later RMs were not fitted with this feature. All photos by Geoff Rixon

Right: Again just ex-works, but this is Edmonton's RCL2245 in October 1980 at Dalston on route 149. All but one of the RCLs, built in 1965 for Green Line routes in Essex and Hertfordshire, were overhauled at Aldenham and used as red buses to accelerate the replacement of Daimler Fleetlines from crew work. The last RCLs were withdrawn from bus work in 1984.

Above: *Not a 2002 Golden Jubilee view, but Turnham Green's RM1983 in June 1983 painted gold to celebrate 50 years of London Transport. It is seen at Feltham on route 237 as Concorde flies overhead.*

Below: *One of the 50 London buses liveried in gold for the Queen's Golden Jubilee in 2002 was Arriva's RM6, seen in August of that year passing Queen Elizabeth Gate, on Park Lane on route 137. Unlike the newer Golden Jubilee buses, which had their gold livery applied rather unattractively in vinyl, Brixton's RM6 was painted.*

*Twenty-five years earlier, London Transport had painted 25
Routemasters in this silver livery and temporarily renumbered them
SRM1-25. At Tottenham Court Road in August 1977 is SRM19, actually
RM1904. Each of the buses was sponsored – this one by Nescafé.*

Above: *The move in recent years to overall advertisements on buses was started in 1969 when RM1737 appeared in a scheme advertising Silexine Paints. This was followed by a spate of other overall-liveried buses, including RM971, promoting Yellow Pages, as seen here on route 11 at Liverpool Street station in 1974.*

Below: *The initial enthusiasm for overall adverts had diminished by the mid-1970s, but RM1237 appeared in this red scheme promoting 200 years of the toothbrush, in 1979. It is seen working out of Palmers Green on route 29 at Trafalgar Square in May 1979.*

Above: *The last overall advert bus for some years was Willesden's RML2492, which ran in this livery promoting film processing at Underwood – when a print cost just 9p. It is seen at the centre-road stand at Marble Arch in July 1984.*

Below: *A different type of overall advert, promoting McDonald's on Original London Sightseeing Tour open-top Routemaster RCL2243, turning into Haymarket from Coventry Street in June 1993.*

Above: *Several London garages kept 'showbus' vehicles, usually with individual features, that were kept in particularly good condition for attendance at rallies and other events. Norwood's RML2270, seen in Park Lane in August 1981 on the 137 route, carries an unusual combination of fleetnames as well as other special touches. Note the poster promoting the GLC's flat-fare scheme.*

Below: *To mark the wedding of Prince Charles and Lady Diana Spencer in July 1981, eight sponsored 'parcel buses' were produced and ran for a few months in this livery. Hammersmith's RM534 is seen on its first day in service in this guise, 15 June 1981, at Butterwick bus station on route 73.*

Above: *The 150th anniversary of George Shillibeer's original horse-drawn Omnibus was celebrated in 1979 and 12 Routemasters were painted in this ornate livery, worn here by Palmers Green's RM2160 at Victoria on route 29 in March 1979.*

Right: *A later London transport anniversary marked the Golden Jubilee of the formation of the London Passenger Transport Board in 1933. In addition to gold-painted RM1983, seen on page 34, there were four RMs painted in the livery worn by LPTB buses in 1933. Chalk Farm's RM1933 is at Pimlico in August 1983.*

Left: *One hundred of the longer RMLs were allocated to London Transport's Country Area for bus work in 1965/6. Godstone's RML2349 is seen at Bromley North station on route 410 in the summer of 1966.*

Below: *After a nearly a decade in service with LT's Country Area successor, London Country, most of the LCBS Routemasters were repurchased by London Transport, for service work or as training buses. Leatherhead's RMC1480 is seen in Surbiton in June 1978 on the 406 route. Passengers apparently had a choice of London Country/Green Line Golden Rover tickets, or the National Wanderbus ticket of LCBS's parent group, National Bus Company.*

THE FIRST FLEETLINES

GEOFF O'BRIEN pictures recall early versions of Daimler's famous rear-engined chassis

THE FLEETLINE was Daimler's last great success, a rear-engined double-deck chassis with a Gardner engine to please the engineers and accountants and a drop-centre rear axle to allow normal seating on both decks. Although it was beaten on to the market by the Leyland Atlantean, the Fleetline soon caught up and became the model of choice in the city fleets in Birmingham and London, and while London may have lived to regret it, Birmingham apparently had no real problems. It was also found in BET and SBG fleets, as well with in a range of municipal and independent operators.

Introduced in 1960, it took a couple of years for Fleetline production to build up, but after that there was no stopping it. Later in its life there were longer Fleetlines, single-deck Fleetlines and even Leyland Fleetlines, but Geoff's photos concentrate on early Fleetline deliveries when it was a defiantly Daimler double-deck chassis. **CB**

The earliest body designs on rear-engined double-deckers were far from inspired. This is one of Birmingham City Transport's 1962 prototype batch of CRG6LX Fleetlines with Metro-Cammell bodies, seen in later West Midlands PTE days in Coventry in 1978, in the company of front-engined Daimler CVG6s. All photos by Geoff O'Brien

Above: *Northern Counties managed a stylish and solid look for their first Fleetline bodies, like Lancashire United no.173 of 1964, seen here arriving in St Helens on the former South Lancashire trolleybus service from Atherton, complete with conductor (or guard) on the front platform.*

Above: *The first Fleetlines built by East Lancs were for Warrington Corporation and had this rather flat design of coachwork that was greatly improved by the commendably deep windows. New in 1963, no.23 was one of a batch of nine delivered that year.*

The Warrington-style body from East Lancs developed into this design with two-piece curved windscreen, as shown by Coventry Corporation no.17, new in 1966, in Pool Meadow bus station.

Above: *West Bromwich Corporation chose both Eastern Coach Works and Metro-Cammell to body its Fleetlines. Lowheight ECW-bodied no.119 is seen in West Midlands PTE days, in 1976.*

Below: *Scottish Bus Group companies went to Alexander, ECW and Northern Counties for its Fleetline bodies, all lowheight buses. ECW-bodied MRF111 of Alexander (Midland) is seen in 1978.*

Above: *After many years of building its own double-deckers in-house, Midland Red turned to the Daimler Fleetline, and one of the 1968 batch is seen leaving Birmingham's Bull Ring bus station. Their Alexander bodies, based on the style developed first for Glasgow Corporation, were unique in having flat-glass front screens on both decks.*

Left: *A rarity – one of the two MH Cars-bodied Fleetlines diverted to the Bournemouth fleet from a Belfast Corporation order. No.40 is being turned on the famous trolleybus turntable at Christchurch.*

ON OTHER PAGES

Colour photographs that link with the articles in this book

Above: **The Brighton Road** *Michael Baker recalls journeys to Brighton on Southdown Leyland Tiger coaches like this splendid preserved 1937 TS7 with Harrington coachwork.* Michael H C Baker

Left: *The famous preserved Brighton Corporation 1939 AEC Regent/ Weymann, FUF 63, wears the livery shared with Brighton, Hove & District, right down to the fleetname.* Michael H C Baker

Above: **Classic Wonderbus** Built for United Auto in 1973 for its express services between the North East of England and London, this 12m Bristol REMH6G with Plaxton bodywork was in the Bristol-friendly fleet of Northern Bus when photographed at Meadowhall in August 1995.
Gavin Booth

Below: Citybus/Ulsterbus received the last Bristol REs, and a few survivors remain in stock as this is written. In Belfast in June 1996 is Citybus no.2533, an RELL6G with Alexander (Belfast) body, placed in service in 1983.
Gavin Booth

Top: **Checkpoint – CIÉ's M-class Leopards** *CIÉ 12m Leyland Leopard no.MG58, the G signifying the Detroit Diesel (General Motors) re-engining. It is seen at Dublin's Busaras bus station in April 1980.*
Gavin Booth

Above: **The Economic Bus Service** *The Economic name and colours were revived by Busways in the 1980s. Leyland Atlantean AN68A/2R no.274 with Alexander 86-seat body sits in South Shields in April 1989, though it is not operating a former Economic service.*
Gavin Booth

Top: **The Last Thing on my Mind** *An unknown notable of the Valleys does his best to add to the photograph of a Rhondda AEC Regent V/Weymann by imitating the pose of the incongruous and almost-Parisian-and-unsuitable fin-de-siècle statue in otherwise pretty bleak surroundings.*
Robert E Jowitt

Above: **Checkpoint – Trent Motor Traction** *The very last traditional Leyland bus body was mounted on this 1954 Titan PD2/12 for Trent, now fortunately preserved. It had been brought out of storage for an Omnibus Society party in 1975, hence the dust.*
Gavin Booth

Born: Leyland, Lancashire, 1970.

Parents: Leyland Truck & Bus and Coras Iompair Éireann, the Irish state transport company.

What was it?: The PSU5/4R – the 12m version of the 11-year-old Leyland Leopard. Although sister company AEC was quick off the mark in getting newly legalised 12m coaches into a few British coach fleets, it is some sign of Leyland's weaker position at this end of the domestic coach market that its first success with the stretched Leopard was in the export market closest to home. A few early examples went to the British Overseas Airways Corporation (the long-haul half of what soon became British Airways) and Weardale Motor Services, but CIÉ showed most faith with an order for 213 that in other circumstances would have been the first of 1,000 or more.

What were these other circumstances?: CIÉ went off Leyland in a big way, but, ironically, that prolonged the lives of many of the 213 and, in any case, don't you want to know more about them?

Okay, so what were they called?: They were CIÉ's M class, continuing a less-than-logical alphanumerical fleetnumbering system that had its roots in Alexander's prewar system in Scotland.

Eh?: An Alexander's man called Bisset became rolling stock engineer at Dublin United Tramways in 1936 and imported his previous employer's fleetnumbering system. Indeed, it's been suggested that Alexander's SMT parent group may have had a financial stake in DUT, but that is a tad irrelevant as DUT and its fleet-numbering system were amalgamated into CIÉ in 1945. Just as in Scotland, Leyland Tigers were a P class and, when they arrived, Titans were an R class. At the time, the M class comprised just one Guy. While Alexander's got complicated postwar and called its PS1 and PS2 Tigers PA and PB, had PC-class Royal Tigers, PD-class Tiger Cubs and PE-class Leopards, CIÉ's postwar Tigers were still Ps and Royal Tigers were U (for underfloor?), re-using a letter DUT first applied to prewar Internationals. Spookily, before any Alexander fleets got PE-class Leopards, CIÉ called its first examples class E (the original DUT E class comprising 45 Dennis Es). They were followed by newer Leopards of mixed length, which became the C class (DUT had seven C-class AECs). Maybe the 12m Leopards were M for 'metre' or 'metric' as they were the first generation of vehicles measured in metric rather than imperial; Bristol's 12m RE coach was the REMH, following the 32ft RESH (short) and 36ft RELH (long). But don't count on it as its Bombardiers were in a K class, which stood for Knothing at all.

And who built the bodies?: CIÉ, in its Spa Road works in Dublin. As had become its practice by then, they were assembled from Metal Sections kits built in the West Midlands and they were to quite a striking, unique design. When new, they were used on a mixture of long-distance scheduled services and on extended tours and had up to 55 seats.

And what was this falling-out with Leyland?: Like many British operators, CIÉ was on the receiving end of a manufacturer that took its customers for granted, was sometimes slow in responding to their problems and in supplying essential spare parts, and had little domestic competition. This apparently boiled over into a huge face-to-face row between CIÉ and Leyland top management and, as an operator that wasn't bound by the patriotic ties that hobbled the British public-sector fleets, it resolved to place its business elsewhere.

And that was where?: Initially with Van Hool, later with Bombardier and GAC, all of whom became involved in various CIÉ ventures to build buses to the operator's own specification in Ireland. To begin with, that revolved around General Motors Detroit Diesel engines and Allison transmission and none of it was immensely successful, but it did give Leyland the bloody nose that it deserved and it prolonged the M class's lives in imaginative ways.

Which were?: By giving them new engines and, in some cases, gearboxes. While CIÉ struggled to get the Irish bus manufacturing business into existence, it didn't receive a single new bus. So it re-engined many of the M class. It started with the most drastic move, turning 100 members of the M class into an MG class, with the Detroit/Allison driveline inserted into radically modified chassis frames. There also were MD-class rebuilds, with Leyland-derived DAF engines plonked into otherwise largely unaltered chassis.

And how long did this life extension last?: In some cases until 2002, long after the last Bombardier coaches and many GAC single-deckers had departed the Bus Éireann fleet formed out of CIÉ. These last models ran mainly as rural school buses and their number included some still powered by Leyland 680 engines, which suggests the original model was a lot better than the operator thought 30 years earlier. But then they also outlasted their manufacturer.

Alan Millar

The length of the M-class Leopards is obvious in this CIÉ publicity shot taken at Bantry Bay.
Bus Éireann

COACHBUILDING

MIKE FENTON tells how a yachtbuilder turned to coachbuilding

IN THE PAST, a number of British seaside towns accommodated bus and coach bodybuilders, production often being undertaken in the winter months and providing employment for otherwise idle coach drivers. Some of the best-known names of the coachbuilding industry were to be found on the coast, for example H V Burlingham in Blackpool and Thos Harrington in Hove. Many of the smaller coachbuilders also fell into this category such as Devon Coachbuilders, which was based in Torquay, Watson's in Lowestoft and Spicer in Southport, to name but three. Despite recent cutbacks Plaxton, of course, maintains the tradition in the Yorkshire resort of Scarborough, but there was also a significant coachbuilding industry a few miles down the coast in the town of Bridlington between 1947 and 1952, started by a company with the unlikeliest of names – Yorkshire Yachtbuilders!

The business was formed by two members of the Royal Yorkshire Yacht Club – Ernest Hartley, a brass founder from Sheffield, and Norman Cooke, a shoddy manufacturer from the West Riding of Yorkshire –

and was registered in 1939 as the Yorkshire Yacht Building and Engineering Co Ltd, for the purpose of servicing boats in the area. A site was leased from Bridlington Borough Council at Clough Hole at the west end of the harbour but, with the outbreak of war, the company's efforts were redirected and wooden vessels built to serve the naval bases and anchorages that had come into being as a result of the conflict. The company also built Admiralty and air-sea rescue launches during the war as well as cobles for local fishermen. At this time the Managing Director and Company Secretary was a man by the name of Butcher, with Jack Munn as Works Manager, both having previously been employed by the British Power Boat Co Ltd, Southampton.

As the war drew to an end in 1945, the company was still engaged in boatbuilding but also actively seeking other work and applied to run a 50-odd-seater 'Sea Coach' service from the South Foreshore to Flamborough calling also at Bridlington Harbour, North Foreshore and Danes Dyke, but the application was withdrawn in December of that year

N BRIDLINGTON

after protests from other parties, including East Yorkshire Motor Services Ltd. By this time, the original West End yard had been augmented by additional premises rented from Williamson's, the Bridlington bus operator, and it was this address, in Havelock Place, which now appeared on the company's literature.

Significant

A more significant occurrence in 1945 was the General Election when Mr George Wadsworth, a Halifax varnish and paint manufacturer, was elected Liberal Member of Parliament for the local Buckrose parliamentary division. At the same time, local elections for the Council of the Borough of Bridlington resulted in the Progressive Party returning several candidates intent on developing light industry in the town, one of these individuals being Jack Munn of Yorkshire Yachtbuilders. As a consequence, the council acquired by compulsory purchase a ten-acre site adjacent to Bessingy Road on the western edge of the town – the land having been owned by Mrs B Wright of Bessingby Hall – and named it the Bessingby Industrial Estate.

Above left: A view inside the works in Yorkshire Equipment days, showing a number of prewar, Roe-bodied AEC Regents of Leeds in varying stages of rebuilding.
Mike Fenton collection

Above: One of the earliest Yorkshire Yacht bodies was fitted to HTD 75, the coach going to Robinson's of Great Harwood near Blackburn in May 1947. Later bodies by this builder had a more prominent side flash and curved, rather than flat, panelling above the side windows. It was rebodied by Duple and reregistered MTH 636 in 1956.
Mike Fenton collection

The year 1946 was one of mixed fortunes for the company. It began badly when it received notice to vacate its West End site and this resulted in the opening of negotiations with the council for new premises at Langdales Wharf. Better news was the receipt of an order for customs patrol boats from Beirut valued at more than £10,000 for completion that year. Unfortunately, following delivery of the first, it was found that the Lebanese Government would not forward payment until all eight had been supplied. This put the company in considerable

As Yorkshire Equipment, the company continued production of coach bodies, producing another 24 of similar appearance. One of these was JXL 603, a Daimler CVD6 which, despite the registration, was new to the Co-operative Travel Service, Manchester in July 1948. In 1957 it left these shores for the Spanish island of Gran Canaria and the AICASA fleet with which it ran for several more years as GC-10952.
PM Photography

financial difficulty and a decision was made to convert the remaining vessels into two-berth cabin cruisers, all of which were eventually sold following the placing of advertisements in various yachting journals.

In July 1946, Mr L M (George) Garwood was appointed as assistant to Mr Munn and soon discovered the financial state of the company to be precarious. He persuaded the recently-elected George Wadsworth MP to visit the works and he, in turn, contacted his friend Donald Holdsworth of Halifax, who was a director of a number of companies in the Holdsworth & Hanson group. Donald Holdsworth and his father Charles both took shares in Yorkshire Yachbuilders to give financial support and were appointed directors of the company. Jack Munn was dismissed on return from his holiday in August 1946 with George Garwood appointed in his place as the new Managing Director and Company Secretary. Other changes also included the retirement of Ernest Hartley, thus ending the link with the founders, Norman Cooke having left the company in the previous year. In the meantime council approval had been given to the move to Langdales Wharf but, with the Bessingby Industrial Estate proposed, that seemed a better prospect and an application was submitted for a three-acre plot there on a 99-year lease. This was taken-up on 16 December 1946 by O&C Estates Ltd, 'O' and 'C' in the title being the brothers Oliver and Charles Holdsworth.

Disastrous

Private yacht building was proving to be disastrous with inadequate costing and inefficient working practices resulting in craft being sold at a loss and causing the company to edge ever closer to bankruptcy. At the same time however, companies in the Holdsworth & Hanson group, like many others, urgently required luxury coach bodies so the directors agreed to a radical change of direction and to utilise their expertise in coachbuilding. One of the companies in the group was Robinson's of Great Harwood and Alan Robinson of that concern was actively involved in designing the bodies, specifying very deep windows and Christie-Tyler aircraft-type reclining seats. Mr J S Lees was appointed Sales Manager and a draughtsman recruited from Eastern Coach Works was given the task of preparing drawings for the new venture. Although it was obvious from the drawings that the size of window chosen would expose passengers' legs to view, a prototype body was still constructed to that design. However, following

The building of coach bodies by Yorkshire Equipment had ceased by the end of 1948 with the construction of East Lancs-style bus bodywork taking over. Rotherham Corporation was one of two main customers with no.200, a Bristol K6B new in December 1949, being a good example.
Mike Fenton

completion, sanity prevailed and the idea was abandoned, with subsequent bodies built to a more conventional style having shallower windows.

Production bodies, like the prototype, were to be built on Daimler CVD6 chassis supplied by Holdsworth & Hanson but, as supplies of these were delayed, a number of goods bodies were sub-contracted from Oswald Tillotson Ltd, also a company in the group, to provide work in the interim. Production of coach bodies got underway as soon as the Daimler chassis arrived in 1947, the first examples being built alongside goods bodies and boats in the old, cramped premises in Havelock Place.

Hangars

Meanwhile, on the Bessingby Estate, a prefabricated steel-framed building, clad in asbestos sheet, had been erected during the first half of 1947. This comprised six ex-RAF blister hangars placed end-to-end providing an impressive workshop some 270ft in length by 85ft in width and this was occupied towards the end of the year. Up to that time most of the small number of bodies built had been for

Robinson's but, following visit by Daimler's northern sales manager, Mr W L Drummond, orders were taken from several other customers desperate for coaches.

By the end of 1947, vehicle bodybuilding had completely taken over and the company's days as builders of marine craft were at an end. To reflect this change of production, the name of the business was changed in January 1948 to the Yorkshire Equipment Company Ltd. The 'new' company maintained a strong Halifax contingent with directors Charles and Donald Holdsworth and George Craven, former General Manager at Halifax, who had initially worked as a consultant, as well as George Wadsworth who had been a director of Yorkshire Yachtbuilders. Craven had wide connections in the bus-operating industry and this resulted in considerable rebuilding work being obtained from a number of Yorkshire-based fleets, including the corporations of Leeds, Hull, and Rotherham as well as East Yorkshire Motor Services and Bullock's of Wakefield. In order to cope with this work, Craven appointed his former body-shop superintendent from Halifax, Leslie Boulton, as Works Manager.

Rebuilding

As well as undertaking the thorough rebuilding of many dilapidated single- and double-deck bodies, the company continued the production of coach bodies to the distinctive halfcab, half-canopy Yorkshire Yachtbuilders style, another 24 being supplied on Daimler CVD6 chassis during 1948. One other

No.BR28 is typical of 30 Albion Venturer CX19 buses rebodied by East Lancs (Bridlington) for Glasgow Corporation from 1950 onwards. Managing director Mr George Garwood can be seen at the extreme left of the group of dignitaries 'waving off' the bus.
Mike Fenton collection

vehicle dealt with by Yorkshire Equipment was DT 4148, a former Doncaster Corporation Dennis Lancet I of 1933, rebodied for Beehive Services of Adwick-le-Street and notable in being the only coach body built on a non-Daimler chassis. It has also been suggested that a body was built on a Seddon Mark 4 chassis for Norfolk independent Yaxley & Sayer of Great Yarmouth but no evidence has been forthcoming to support this claim. Certainly the Seddon existed (EX 6410) but photographs show it having a Plaxton body of the style expected on a 1949 Seddon and George Garwood has no recollection of the company bodying such a chassis.

Unfortunately it must be said that durability of the coach bodies was not their best feature. They were described, disparagingly, by one operator with first-hand knowledge, as having 'lots of timber in them, but in the wrong places'! This is underlined by the statistic that of the 34 Daimler CVD6 chassis bodied by Yorkshire Yachtbuilders and Yorkshire Equipment, more than a third received new bodies within eight years with one example rebodied after just four! Notable exceptions were JXL 603 and SML 475 which survived long enough to be exported to the Canary Islands in 1956 and the AICASA fleet of Gran Canaria where they ran for another ten years or more as GC-10952 and GC-10438 respectively, outlasting their siblings by a considerable margin! In fairness, structural problems were not unknown on many of the products of the smaller postwar coachbuilders, whose lack of design experience

coupled with poor quality timber often led to early rebuilding or rebodying.

In the meantime Rotherham Corporation had several orders in hand with East Lancashire Coachbuilders, but delivery was limited by the size of the Blackburn premises. Rotherham's General Manager, Norman Rylance, had visited the Yorkshire Equipment works with his chief engineer to inspect rebuilding work being carried out on his undertaking's vehicles and, being satisfied with what he had seen, suggested arrangements might be made for vehicles from the Rotherham order to be built at Bridlington. After some discussion East Lancashire agreed to the Bridlington company acting as sub-contractors, steel frames being supplied from Blackburn at cost plus a profit mark-up and the bodies built under licence. This arrangement commenced around springtime in 1949, the Bridlington-built bodies being indistinguishable from the native East Lancashire products. By this time the building of coach bodies had ceased and a substantial order by Holdsworth & Hanson for a further 52 CVD6 chassis from Daimler was cancelled.

From mid-1949 to mid-1950, Aldershot & District placed in service a total of 30 Dennis Lance K3 with GAA or GOU registrations, a dozen of which were bodied by Yorkshire Equipment with the remainder built in Blackburn. All had lowbridge, 51-seat, five-bay bodies as illustrated by no.125 in Guildford bus station.
Photobus

Greater control

As the sub-contract bodybuilding arrangement progressed, the directors of East Lancashire sought greater control over the work being built in Yorkshire, as well as greater financial benefit, so, following further negotiations, Yorkshire Equipment was completely taken over and renamed East Lancashire Coachbuilders (Bridlington) Ltd in March 1950. The new company's directors were those of Yorkshire Equipment plus Walter Smith, Alfred Alcock and George Danson from Blackburn. The Blackburn company sent one of its foremen, Jack Newsome, to supervise construction and soon afterwards Works Manager Leslie Boulton left to return to his original post in Halifax, having not settled in Bridlington. The position of Works Manager was then filled by Dennis Flavell, assisted by Jack Newsome.

In view of the volume of work in hand, it was decided to erect a second building, similar to and alongside the first, thus taking up a second acre of land, this being completed early in 1951. Around the same time, it had been agreed that the company could tender independently for contracts rather than relying solely on work emanating from Blackburn. As a consequence, several orders for van bodywork were obtained from companies in the North and East Ridings of Yorkshire with construction taking place during that year. Other non-passenger bodywork built at this time also included the fitting of new cabs and flat beds on older wagon chassis acquired by British Road Services following the

Although Preston lies only ten miles to the west of Blackburn, it was Yorkshire Equipment that provided 35-seat rear entrance bus bodies on a pair of Leyland Tiger PS1 chassis for that undertaking in 1949, Preston no.75 being shown.
Mike Fenton collection

nationalisation of road transport in 1948.

During his parliamentary career, director George Wadsworth had made many contacts, including a man called Johnson, who was principal director of a company manufacturing cabinets for radio and television sets. Furthermore, the sales manager of that company, who had previously been employed by the Educational Supplies Association, advised there was a great demand for school furniture and this could offer significant opportunities for a new supplier. The directors of the old Yorkshire Equipment Co were aware of their dependency on bus bodybuilding and, furthermore, that these bodies were being built under an agreement which, if circumstances changed, could leave the factory with no work. They therefore thought it wise to diversify into other areas of manufacture and, with this in mind, schools were visited to study requirements and prototype desks, chairs, tables and cupboards constructed. Convinced of the viability of this activity, a new company was registered in the late summer of 1951 as the Yorkshire Equipment Co (1951) Ltd.

Furniture manufacturing was undertaken in another factory on the opposite side of Bessingby

From March 1950 onwards, production continued as East Lancashire Coachbuilders (Bridlington) Ltd, some of the bodies built under this title in the first year being nine 56-seat rebodies on wartime Guy Arab II chassis for Burnley, Colne & Nelson. The same operator also had a batch of Guy Arab III buses new in 1951 which have always been recorded as bodied at Blackburn, but an official view of AHG 640 posed in exactly the same location as the Arab II suggests some, if not all, of this batch were supplied by the Bridlington factory.
Mike Fenton collection

Road in premises of the associated Bessingby Engineering Co Ltd. Although the activities of the new company were as stated, bodybuilding skills were still present and utilised to construct a pantechnicon body on 1936 Bristol JO5G ET 9627, formerly of Rotherham Corporation. This was the only body of any kind built by the company and the vehicle was used solely for deliveries to schools etc, the previously used British Railways service having proving unsatisfactory.

Buyer

Although orders continued to flow in to the various companies, Charles Holdsworth's enthusiasm for the business had waned as the years had passed. He was now in his seventies, both his sons had emigrated to South Africa and he had little desire to continue the business in Bridlington. The prospect of any significant financial return was now remote and George Craven was therefore instructed to find a buyer. A meeting was arranged with William Black – later Lord Black – Managing Director of Park Royal Vehicles, and Holdsworth, Craven and Garwood all travelled to London for discussions regarding the take-over of the business by Park Royal. However that company was experiencing problems of its own at this time, the postwar boom was nearing its end, orders were decreasing and nothing resulted from the talks.

Having failed to attract a buyer, in June 1952 all the Bridlington companies were put into voluntary liquidation with George Smith, of Smith & Garton of Huddersfield, appointed as liquidator. A small number of bodies in hand, on prewar Rotherham Bristol L5G chassis, were completed as far as framing was concerned, then sent in skeleton form to S H Bond of Wythenshawe, Manchester for finishing and the balance of a large Glasgow order was transferred to Blackburn. As a result of this action and through no fault of their own, 200 hundred workers in the bodybuilding and furniture-making factories became unemployed, and Bridlington's only manufacturer of any size was no more.

At the start of 1953, the factory was still occupied by a token staff but was finally vacated following a

Above: *Rotherham also had eight 38-seat trolleybus bodies built by Yorkshire Equipment on Daimler CTC6 and CTE6 chassis during 1949 and 1950 (as well as others built under the East Lancashire name). The former FET 344 is seen later in its career in 1967 after export to Spain when operating for Tranvia de San Sebastián a Tolosa, its body rebuilt as a 21-seater with separate entrance and exit on the old offside in place of the central entrance it had in England.*
Mike Fenton collection

Below: *East Lancs (Bridlington) continued to body trolleybuses but, unlike Yorkshire Equipment, also included double-deckers, a total of 15 bodies being built on Sunbeam F4 chassis during 1950/1. Seven were for Tees-side Railless Traction and the balance of eight were 55-seaters for St Helens Corporation, all of which were withdrawn in 1958 and sold to South Shields as demonstrated by no.207.*
Mike Fenton collection

Rotherham proved to be the best customer for Bridlington-built East Lancs bodies and took the only Bristol KS chassis not to be bodied by ECW, a batch of 12 KS6B of 1950/1. Typical was no.104, new in January 1951 and seen some 16 years later near the town centre with a nice selection of 1960s traffic in the background.
Mike Fenton

sale by auction of all remaining wood and metal-working equipment, tools and stocks, this taking place during 14-16 April 1953. The premises were then leased by O&C Estates Ltd to the Ministry of Supply for use as a food store, these having been set up at various points around the country in order to provide essential supplies in case of a national emergency, for example further warfare.

Wide range

During five years of production, the business had built luxury coaches for independent operators and followed these with bodies for single- and double-deck motorbuses and trolleybuses on a wide range of chassis, mostly but not exclusively for the municipal sector. Exceptions included BET company Aldershot & District, which had several Yorkshire-Equipment-bodied Dennis Lances, and the Golden Arrow fleet in South Africa, for which bodies were constructed on at least two Leyland OPD2/1 chassis. As far as can be ascertained, Yorkshire Yacht was responsible only for the first ten bodies, with Yorkshire Equipment building over 50 more and East Lancs (Bridlington) contributing at least another 100 to the total. It should be noted that numbers bodied by the last two companies are not easy to define, as several bodies recorded simply as East Lanc, are thought also to have been built in Yorkshire.

Until the early 1990s the premises were still in existence, having been occupied by a variety of companies, but all had gone by the middle of that decade, with the inevitable supermarket now occupying part of the site. By a strange coincidence though, buses can again be found there, as the estate currently hosts East Yorkshire Motor Services' Bridlington allocation.

In conclusion, I would like to express my gratitude to all those individuals who have in some way contributed to this short history, but singled out for special thanks is former Managing Director George Garwood, whose detailed knowledge of the day-to-day running of the business has provided a wealth of fascinating and previously unrecorded information. The story would have been much the poorer were it not for his contribution and I am very grateful to him for all his help. Finally, I would also like to mention the PSV Circle's excellent publications, which have proved to be a valuable source of information concerning vehicles bodied in Bridlington. **CB**

A 40-YEAR LOVE-AFFAIR

GAVIN BOOTH tells the story of Edinburgh Corporation Transport's long association with Daimlers

EDINBURGH CORPORATION liked its Daimlers. And, it can be assumed, Daimler liked Edinburgh Corporation. Between 1928 and 1950 Edinburgh Corporation (ECT) bought just short of 300 Daimlers, and for several years before World War 2 it bought nothing else. On the evidence of 20 years of regular purchases, Daimler might reasonably have expected ECT to continue to buy Daimlers, right through tin-front CVG6s and Fleetlines; after all, Scotland's other three municipal fleets, Aberdeen, Dundee and Glasgow, did – even if Glasgow's Fleetline intake amounted to just one fairly under-used bus.

So what went wrong? In two words, Moris Little.

When he took over as ECT's Transport Manager in 1948 he had other ideas. As an engineer he doubtless knew the value of that rugged slogger of an engine, the Gardner, that was fitted to the Daimlers he inherited. But he turned to Leylands and never really looked back.

Daimler was always a well-regarded bus chassis maker, and although in the 1920s it seemed well able

A fine line-up of Daimlers in Edinburgh Corporation's Central Garage, featuring several of the 1930 batch of Daimler CF6s with Cowieson bodies.
Gavin Booth collection

to produce fine chassis, it never quite found the right engine to match.

ECT's first Daimlers, although built by Daimler at Coventry, were strictly Associated Daimlers – ADCs – products of the short-lived liaison between AEC and Daimler. Before 1928 ECT's buses were AECs, Dennises, Karriers and Leylands, so the eight ADC 423s with 32-seat two-door Edinburgh-built Croall bodies were interesting purchases. The 423 chassis had Daimler's 3.568-litre CV25 petrol engine, not a particularly well-regarded unit. The next year ECT bought AEC Reliances and Leyland Lions – plus one Daimler CF6; this was a happier model, with Daimler's new 5.76-litre CV35 petrol engine, and in 1930 there followed a further 36 CF6s. The 1929 prototype had a 32-seat Croall body, but the 1930 buses had 32-seat bodies by Cowieson, of Glasgow. Fourteen more CF6s followed in 1931, with 31-seat bodies by Alexander Motors of Edinburgh.

Current models

At the same time as ECT was taking delivery of its CF6s, it was receiving examples of other models in an effort to find a new standard supplier. Late in 1930 it placed a Hume-bodied Daimler CH6 in service, its first bus with fluid flywheel and preselector gearbox. In 1931 there was an Albion PMB28, a Crossley Alpha, three Morris Dictators and a rare Daimler CG6. There would be no further orders for Albion or Crossley for many years, but the

Morris enjoyed a brief period of popularity in Edinburgh; between 1930 and 1934, ECT bought 23 Morrises, before the company pulled out of heavy bus production.

The 1931 Daimler CG6 had a 31-seat Alexander Motors body, to ECT's current two-door (front and rear) standard. The CG6 was a short-lived model, essentially an improved CF6, and Edinburgh's example is believed to be the only one bodied as a single-decker.

The first part of Daimler's big step forward came with the adoption of fluid-flywheel transmission with the Wilson preselective epicyclic gearbox, allowing drivers to preselect gears at a suitable time and change gear by pressing the change pedal, which replaced the normal clutch pedal. The first bus chassis with the preselective gearbox was the CH6, introduced in 1930, and ECT took a batch of nine in 1932, fitted with 30-seat Cowieson bodies with rear entrances, the first of what would become the new standard single-deck body layout.

Just one Daimler came to ECT in 1933, a CP6 with English Electric 34-seat front entrance body. The CP6 was a development of the CH6 with a new

poppet-valve engine in place of the older sleeve-valve CV35 unit.

Diesel engines

By this time diesel engines were beginning to find increasing favour with bus operators, and in 1934 ECT started by fitting diesels into some of its older petrol-engined buses, including AEC Reliances, the

Top: *Edinburgh had only one Daimler CP6, no.4970M with English Electric body. New in 1933, it received a Gardner 5LW diesel engine in 1935 and survived until 1952.*
Gavin Booth collection

Above: *G25 from Edinburgh's first batch of Daimler COG6 with Metropolitan-Cammell bodies, in Annandale Street. Between 1935 and 1939 ECT received a total of 51 similar double-deckers.*
Roy Marshall

Top: *When some of the COG6s were rebuilt by ECT they were given a more modern appearance by removing the rain deflectors above the windows, and fitting the standard destination display of the time. Half-drop windows gave way to plain glass, with ventilators only on the front windows.*
Gavin Booth collection

Above: *The single-deck equivalent of Edinburgh's standard COG6s were the 65 COG5s with Weymann bodies received between 1936 and 1938. No.A53 is seen in original condition on Waverley Bridge.*
Roy Marshall

Albion and the Crossley. The AECs and the Crossley received diesel engines built by their chassis makers, but the Albion received a Gardner 5LW unit, as did the Albion, the 1930 Daimler CH6, the 1932 CH6s and the 1933 CP6. Another of the CF6s received a Thornycroft diesel at the same time.

By 1934 Daimler had introduced its new CO range of chassis, all with preselective gearboxes and most with Gardner engines. ECT took two new Daimlers that year, a COT4 with Tangye diesel engine and Roberts 32-seat body and a COG5 with Weymann

Top: *When some of the COG5s were rebuilt by ECT after the war, they received larger destination indicators, a flush front panel with recessed offside headlamp, and some, like 638 seen here, sliding ventilators in place of half-drop windows.*
Roy Marshall

Above: *Few photos exist of ECT's utility Daimlers with their original bodies. This St Andrew Square photo shows no.63 with no.67 behind. No.63 has a Massey body, showing signs of its 1949 rebuilding, notably the sliding ventilators. No.67 has a Northern Counties body, which again had undergone rebuilding in the early postwar period.*
J C Gillham

34-seat body. The four-cylinder Tangye VM4 engine was replaced the following year with a Gardner 5LW, the COT4 thus becoming a COG5.

The Daimler/Gardner combination must have appealed to ECT for it bought nothing else for the next five years. The first examples of a new standard double-decker appeared in 1935 – 16 Daimler COG6 with Metropolitan-Cammell 54-seat bodies. The COG6 had Gardner's bigger 8.4-litre 6LW engine, and ECT was the first customer for this chassis.

Top: *Six of the 1932 Daimler CH6s were rebodied in 1949 by Alexander, as seen here on A18 on Waverley Bridge. One of the COG5s was rebodied similarly at the same time. These buses lasted in service until 1959.*
Roy Marshall

Above: *The first new single-deckers bought after the war included 10 of these Daimler CVG5 with Metro-Cammell bodies based very much on the prewar deliveries. No.698 is seen in the Lawnmarket.*
Roy Marshall

These were followed by 20 COG5 single-deckers in 1936, with the 7.0-litre Gardner 5LW engine and bodywork by Metropolitan-Cammell's marketing partner, Weymann; the bodies had 36 seats and cutaway rear entrances, a standard that would remain for more than a decade.

The 1937 deliveries were a mix of COG5 single-deckers (10) and COG6 double-deckers (15), and in 1938 there followed a further 35 COG5s and 18 COG6s; two more COG6s arrived earlier in 1939, the last new vehicles delivered before the war. The 65 COG5s and 51 COG6s had considerably modernised the fleet, and allowed withdrawal of older types, including, in 1937, the 1928 ADC 423s and, in 1938/9, the first of the CF6s and the original CH6. Withdrawal of the CF6s continued until 1944.

Wartime deliveries

When ECT received 'unfrozen' and utility buses in 1942 it got buses from five manufacturers – but not one was a Daimler. The Daimler works at Coventry had been severely damaged in November 1940, causing bus production to cease, but late in 1942 it was announced that production was ready to restart at Wolverhampton. One hundred CWG5 chassis were to be built, essentially a wartime version of the COG5, and ECT received two double-deckers with Massey utility bodies in March 1943. Later in the year came another two Massey-bodied utility Daimler

double-deckers, but these were model CWA6 with the 7.7-litre AEC engine, which would become the standard for most wartime Daimlers. Eight more CWA6s with bodies by Massey (one), Northern Counties (four) and Brush (three) followed in 1944, and a further five CWA6s with Brush bodies came in 1945. One of the Brush-bodied CWA6s, G71, was badly damaged in an accident on The Mound in 1945, and re-entered service in 1948 with a single-deck body, possibly from an older bus, possibly built by ECT on a Brockhouse frame. It only lasted in service until 1952, but was not disposed of until 1958.

During the war ECT had the opportunity to acquire two COG5 single-deckers that had been new in 1936/7 to Dundee Corporation but had been requisitioned by the Ministry of Transport in 1940, and were bought from the Ministry of Supply in 1942. These originally had centre-entrance bodies by English Electric and Cowieson, but ECT rebuilt them as rear-entrance buses before they entered service in 1943. Twenty-four of ECT's own COG5s were requisitioned by the Ministry of Transport in 1940/2

This splendid night photo shows a nearly new G150 on night service duties, complete with the black lining-out that was applied to these buses in their early years. The 'Birmingham' Daimlers were Edinburgh Corporation's most numerous Daimlers, and are probably the most fondly remembered.
Gavin Booth collection

In full ECT colours with fleetnumber 800, this is LRW 377, the Daimler Freeline G6H/S with two-door Duple body, seen at the Duple works at Hendon before receiving its registration number. Gavin Booth collection

and repurchased from the Ministry of Supply in 1942-4. Nine of the COG5s that remained operated with producer-gas trailers in 1943/4. Two of the 1938 COG6 double-deckers were loaned to London Transport in 1940/1.

After the war ECT needed buses quickly, and stocked up on Guy Arabs – double-deckers in 1945-7 and single-deckers in 1948. In 1947 it also took five Daimler CVD6 with Northern Counties double-deck bodies. The CVD6 had Daimler's new 8.6-litre CD6 engine, which the chassis maker was pushing hard at the time; another two similar CVD6s followed in 1948. In 1948/9 ECT bought 10 CVG5 with Metropolitan-Cammell single-deck bodies largely to prewar style.

Birmingham Daimlers

ECT's biggest order in the postwar years was for 72 Daimler double-deckers – ten CVD6 and 62 CVG6 – with Metropolitan-Cammell bodies to a very distinctive Birmingham City Transport design, a move to obtain buses quickly. These buses were delivered between February 1949 and June 1950, and were to prove to be Edinburgh's last-ever Daimlers. Soon ECT would turn to Leylands with a vengeance, but this was not the end of the Daimler story in Edinburgh.

Daimler had bombarded ECT with demonstrators in the early postwar years – two CVD6 single-deckers with Willowbrook bodies and a CVD6 with Northern Coachbuilders double-deck body – and while these may have influenced the choice of Daimler engines in 1947-9, the Daimler chassis was falling out of favour under newly appointed Transport Manager, Moris Little.

Daimler kept trying. There was LRW 377, a Daimler Freeline G6H/S with 36-seat two-door Duple body that was loaned in 1952; this was an underfloor-engined single-decker with the type of standee body that Moris Little was known to favour, and it was painted in ECT livery and carried fleetnumber 800. It joined two Leyland demonstrators, 801/2, which had appeared in 1951, but while the Leylands were bought in 1952, the Daimler was returned to Coventry.

By this time the bodies on the prewar standard Daimlers and the wartime deliveries were needing attention. Thirty of the Weymann-bodied COG5s and a number of the COG6s were extensively rebuilt – just short of rebodying – in 1948-52; the rebuilt buses outlasted their unrebuilt brothers. Genuine rebodies were carried out on six of the 1932 CH6s, which were essentially COG5s following the fitting of Gardner 5LW engines, and on one of the 1948 COG5s whose original body had been destroyed by fire. The rebodying was carried out in 1949 by Alexander at Stirling, the first bodies from this manufacturer for ECT and the start of a long relationship.

The utility bodies on some of the 16 remaining wartime Daimlers were needing attention and in 1948/9 four of them received bodies transferred from 1943 utility Guy Arabs, which were receiving new bodies at the time. Six of the others were heavily rebuilt by Brockhouse or Croft, both based in the west of Scotland, around the same time.

Above left: Sixteen of the utility Daimlers received new Alexander bodies in 1954, producing modern-looking buses that would give ECT a further 13 years' good service. No.69 is seen in Princes Street.
Roy Marshall

Left: In 1959 the 16 rebodied Daimler CWG5s received glassfibre Leyland-style fronts, as on 372 in St Andrew Square.
Gavin Booth

Above: One of the demonstrators sent to Edinburgh by Daimler was VKV 99, the CVG6-30 with Gardner 6LX engine and Willowbrook body, seen here at Pilton on the 19 Circle, a favourite for demonstrators.
Gavin Booth

New bodies

A more significant rebuilding involving the 16 utility Daimlers was carried out in 1954, when all received Gardner 5LW engines and new lightweight Alexander bodies with ornate full fronts. In 1959 they were fitted with Leyland-style glassfibre fronts of the type standard on much of the fleet. In this guise they gave good service until 1967, though latterly the 5LW engines were finding some of Edinburgh's hills a bit of a challenge.

Withdrawal of Daimlers had slowed down during the war years, and there were no withdrawals in the early postwar period when ECT was needing every bus it could muster, but as postwar deliveries got into their stride the first of the COG6 double-deckers went, followed by the unrebuilt COG5s and some of the odd one-off Daimlers bought in the 1930s. This process continued until the last of the rebuilt prewar standards were withdrawn. The last COG6s survived until 1956 and the last COG5s until 1959. The single-deckers withdrawn in 1959 included the Alexander-rebodied 1932 CH6s, which had been re-engined as COG5s early in their lives. The COG5s were withdrawn as a result of the arrival of the first 50 Leyland Tiger Cubs with Weymann bodies, bought to replace the ageing single-deck fleet.

The 10 postwar CVG5 single-deckers went in 1960, following the delivery of the second batch of 50 Tiger Cubs, which prompted a clear-out of the remaining front-engined single-deckers.

The early postwar CVD6 double-deckers went in 1960, and the 10 Birmingham-style CVD6s went in 1962 as ECT withdrew older non-standard double-deckers.

The Daimler fleet now comprised the 16 rebodied CWG5s and the balance of the Birmingham-style CVG6s, less a handful withdrawn prematurely following accidents.

Daimler's last attempt to win ECT business – Fleetline demonstrator 565 CRW with Alexander body picks up passengers at the Trinity terminus of the 23 early in 1965.
Gavin Booth

Withdrawals

Serious withdrawals of the Birmingham Daimlers started in 1964, and the last survivors soldiered on until 1967, including no.135, now preserved by the City of Edinburgh Council, and in the care of the Lothian Bus Consortium.

Also withdrawn in 1967 were the 16 rebodied CWG5s, the chassis of which had completed up to 24 years' service.

So, for the first time for nearly 40 years, there were no Daimlers in the ECT fleet. But Daimler was still trying with demonstrators. In 1954 ECT had tried a CLG5 with the prototype lightweight Metro-Cammell Orion body; in 1957 Daimler sent a CVG6 with Willowbrook body; a year later came a 30ft-long CVG6-30, again with Willowbrook body and the prototype Gardner 6LX engine. But none of these found favour with ECT.

Then early in 1965 ECT mounted a comparison test between four current types of double-decker. There was the Leyland Titan PD3, ECT's own standard at the time; the AEC Renown, which was AEC's latest front-engined lowheight model; the Leyland

Atlantean, which everybody assumed ECT would turn to after building up a fleet of over 400 Leyland Titans; and a Daimler Fleetline with Alexander body. Daimler even painted it in pseudo-ECT livery, and while it performed well, and ECT recommended buying 25 Fleetlines and 25 Atlanteans, the transport committee played safe and ordered 25 Atlanteans and 25 Titan PD3s from Leyland.

Daimlers served Edinburgh well over a significant period in ECT's history, when the tramway system was at its height, but increasing numbers of motorbuses were needed to operate services to the expanding city. The peak year for Daimler deliveries was 1938, when 53 were bought; the Daimler fleet peaked at 218 in 1950; the peak year for withdrawals was 1964, when 42 bit the dust. In all, there were 297 Daimlers in the ECT fleet, and no.135 is a fitting reminder of the fine engineering that went into every one. **CB**

CHRIS DREW reaches 444 and 555

444

Aldershot & District made a welcome appearance with an East Lancs-bodied Dennis Loline I and a couple of Guys, the latter make represented also by an Arab III from Southampton (in drawing) and a newer Arab V for Cardiff. Also from Wales came an MCW-clothed Regent V - I make no comment about its looks. More AECs were a Regent III/ Bruce from Eastbourne and a Reliance/Alexander from Premier Travel. There was a Lodekka from United Auto and from the other side of Hadrian's Wall came one of Edinburgh's tram-replacing Metro-Cammell-bodied PD2s (shiver) and Laurie's Atlantean XVA 444, later to go to Central SMT. Finally (but please do keep reading on) there was JJS 444, a Bedford SB from, well, I think you can guess by now.

555

Here were a brace of Atlanteans – one from Maidstone & District with standard MCW body and a Liverpool version looking just a little peaked. Other Leylands included another PD2 for Edinburgh and a Ribble Leopard. Premier provided another Alexander Y-bodied Reliance with a newcomer from Grey-Green in the shape of a Duple Viceroy Bedford VAM. The trolley this time came from Nottingham (drawing). An oddity came in the form of an ECW Queen Mary-style bodied Daimler CVD for Alexander Midland. Yet again, (please don't go to sleep yet), Mitchell's came up with its usual combination for KJS 555.

THE ECONOM

An account of one of the pioneering bus operations in the North East of England, by GEOFF BURROWS

THE NORTH EAST of England, and in particular County Durham, is well-known in transport circles for the large number of independent bus operators that survived despite the presence of two of the large group companies, Northern General Transport and United Automobile Services. One of these independents was unique in that it competed successfully with not only Northern and its subsidiaries but also two very determined municipal operators, South Shields and Sunderland corporations. The company was Economic Bus Service, of Whitburn, and it survived for only a few months short of 50 years.

To a stranger looking at a map of County Durham, it would be easy to dismiss Whitburn, situated on the coast between South Shields to the north and Sunderland to the south, as a former pit village. In fact it is nothing of the sort. Whitburn has great antiquity: the parish church was built in the 13th century and the village centre is arranged in typical Norman long-green style, notable still for its trees,

attractive buildings and pond. The name Whitburn is Saxon in origin, though there are at least two possible meanings. It could either have been 'Hwita Byrgen', the place (Hwita's tumulus) where the Saxon nobleman Hwita was buried, or alternatively 'Kwit-Berne' (white barn). Fishing, agriculture and limestone quarrying were the mainstays of the economy. The Parish of Whitburn also included the village of Marsden two miles to the north, and this was quite separate and distinct from Whitburn village. Marsden village was built when Whitburn Colliery was established in 1874 by the Whitburn Coal Company. The colliery company built the new pit village at the same time, to house the miners and their families.

The first of a number of ACB bodies for Economic is shown here, symbolically posed at Seaburn, at the end of the Sunderland Corporation tram route. Wilson's no.3 was new in September 1946, with an Albion chassis, complete with coach outline and 35 quite comfortable seats.
Whitburn Local History Group collection

BUS SERVICE

Most of the inhabitants came from the Durham coalfields, though some came from as far afield as Wales and Ireland. A railway line to connect the pit with the coaling staithes at Tyne Dock in South Shields was completed in 1878. Passenger trains also operated on the line to carry miners from South Shields to work. These services operated only at 'change of shift' times, and in 1888 the Board of Trade gave permission for the general public to travel on the trains, though few did so because of the awkward times and frequencies. Stations were built at the colliery and Westoe Lane, South Shields, with an intermediate stop at Marsden. The rolling stock consisted of 'cast-offs' from the railway companies in the area, earning for the train the sobriquet 'The Marsden Rattler'. In 1891 the Whitburn colliery was amalgamated into the ownership of the Harton Coal Company, which owned a further four pits in and around South Shields.

Without proper roads for access until 1880, Whitburn could only be reached by a rough track from Cleadon and Boldon, suitable only for horses and walkers, or by sea, whereby large consignments came and went. For example, it is recorded that in 1810 the new rector had his furniture and belongings brought by rowing boat and landed on the beach. The coast, with its cliffs and rocks, became the graveyard for many of the brave sailors and fishermen who served the community.

Trams

In order to reach Sunderland it was necessary to walk along the sandhills and wade across several streams, the largest of which was where Seaburn is now situated. The first road was actually built on these sand dunes in 1866, but in 1880 a permanent road was laid connecting Whitburn with Sunderland. The roads were gradually improved, allowing access for horse-drawn vehicles, and in 1901 Sunderland Corporation electric trams came within a mile of Whitburn, with their terminus at Seaside Lane, known later as Seaburn.

In 1903 Whitburn Parish Council requested that Sunderland Corporation consider extending its tramways to Whitburn, yet despite several proposals

Large by the standards of the day, this little 20-seat Dennis had a Hall Lewis body. New in 1926, it was one of the vehicles that helped Economic to run the competition off the road.
Whitburn Local History Group collection

This Dennis Lancet (UP 7045) was bought new by Anderson in 1932, and remained in the fleet until 1950, though it was probably not used after 1947. The coach-seated body was also built by Dennis.
R L Kell collection

by various parties over the years the trams never reached the village from any direction. The public either walked or rode on the horse traps that plied between Whitburn and the tram terminus. Then in 1907 the North Eastern Railway Company began a motor-bus service between South Shields and Boldon Colliery via Harton and Cleadon. Another service ran from Boldon Colliery to Cleadon, Whitburn and Seaside Lane, so that it was now possible to reach Whitburn by public transport from both Sunderland and South Shields, albeit with a change of vehicle in mid-journey. The first buses were Saurers, but they were sent to Blyth in Northumberland to begin new routes there and were replaced by larger Dürkopp vehicles. In 1912 South Shields Rural District Council complained to the railway company that something should be done about the serious overcrowding of the buses, because the service had become so popular. The NER workshops at York built three double-deck bodies that were then sent to South Shields to be fitted to three of the Dürkopps. By then, the Boldon service had been abandoned, and the buses ran a through route between South Shields, Cleadon, Whitburn and Seaside Lane.

The improvements were short-lived. The Great War which began in 1914 caused a reduction in manpower and a shortage of petrol, and the service was cut back to the short South Shields-Harton section in 1915. The rest of the route to Cleadon and Whitburn was never to be resumed. Once again Whitburn was left to rely on the pony and trap, but as soon as the war ended in 1918 things began to change. With the availability of cheap war-surplus

vehicles, a number of local entrepreneurs began to ply for hire between Whitburn and the Seaside Lane tram terminus.

The term 'ply for hire' is appropriate because the services were run as an 'end-to-end' journey at a fare of 6d. The terminus was at a stand in Whitburn village, and when each vehicle was full it set off non-stop for Seaside Lane. Then the next bus moved onto the stand, in the manner of taxis. Today it is difficult to believe that at busy times as many as 16 people could crowd into the simple box-like bodies mounted on tiny Ford T chassis. One operator, George Puncheon, showed more foresight than most, not only working buses north from Whitburn village to the railway terminus at the colliery but also buying two Napiers with no fewer than 14 seats. Using these, he attracted excursion traffic on sunny days when he ran even further north to the limit of the existing road at Souter Point, where the lighthouse still stands. The time was now ripe for bigger things.

Bus service

Probably over a pint, old friends George Anderson and Teddy Wilson discussed the idea of running a bus service from their home village of Stanley in northwest County Durham to the nearby market town of Chester-le-Street. This was in early 1925,

In 1945 the Government announced that Albion would be permitted to resume bus chassis production. The first 54 Valkyrie CX13 models were built during 1946/7, all with Pickering semi-utility bodies and Albion six cylinder 9.09-litre diesel engines. The Wilson fleet received two in 1946; here is no.2 (FUP 368) in South Shields.
G Burrows

and George Anderson gave up his job as a fitter with Northern General and Edward Wilson also left his work at a colliery in Stanley. Anderson bought a 12-seat Siddeley and Wilson a Reo Speedwagon with 14 seats and they began their new bus service with them. The Siddeley was converted from a five-year-old ambulance, but the Speedwagon seems to have been only a year old. Unfortunately it was involved in an accident within weeks of starting the service, but such was the partners confidence in success that Wilson immediately bought a replacement Reo. Then came the news that the damaged vehicle could in fact be repaired and put back into service, so that they now had a spare vehicle.

Anderson and Wilson took one of their buses to Whitburn on an excursion, and saw the possibilities there for a properly managed bus service. They placed the Reo on the Seaside Lane route and were immediately successful, though its larger capacity caused problems with the established system of working, to the extent that on occasions fights broke out between drivers touting for passengers. The partners took this in their stride in two ways. They first began operating regular through journeys between Whitburn Colliery and Seaside Lane, and then, using Anderson's professional experience from his days with Northern, introduced timetable working. More fights ensued!

General Strike

The next step was to support the local miners and their families in their search for work. A debilitating strike from June to October 1925 was followed by the General Strike in May 1926, after which the owners 'locked out' the miners. The partners realised that a regular service to South Shields would allow the miners to seek alternative work there and also encourage the Whitburn population to make trips to the shops and other facilities. The old NER bus route was out of the question, because Northern and Sunderland District were now operating the Cleadon-Harton-South Shields section as part of their direct service between South Shields and Sunderland. The only alternative was over a level crossing on the colliery railway, for which a toll was paid on every journey, then north up a steep and narrow road to the top of a hill, passing the limestone quarries. The road also belonged to the colliery company, but the toll for this was levied on only one day of every year. Once this hill (known as 'the High Road', though the actual name is Lizard Lane) had been breasted, the road then descended to Horsley Hill, which was then on the outskirts of South Shields.

This then was the chosen route for the Economic buses, as they were now known. Unlike Sunderland, the South Shields authorities allowed the buses to reach the town centre, which they did by way of Harton and Westoe, terminating in Ocean Road adjacent to the busy Fowler Street junction, and only

The ACB service bus body fitted to Anderson's Leyland PS1 no.17 looked well-balanced and businesslike. Of interest is the route number box, fitted on these and similar Economic buses but never used.
R L Kell collection

two minutes' walk to the railway station. The partners realised from the very beginning of this service that a high standard of maintenance was essential for the buses to withstand the rigours of the climb over the Cleadon hills. This became a company tradition, and was one of the reasons for the longevity of many of the buses. Though not steep by today's standards, the 'High Road' was nevertheless a tough climb for the buses of those days. Small boys would often gather at the foot of the hill, ready to give a helping push to reluctant cars and trucks, and even on occasions, an Economic bus.

By using a combination of a regular timetable between South Shields and Sea Lane, larger more comfortable buses and lower fares, and because the bigger buses generated more income at less cost, Economic became the sole operator by 1927. The smaller operators just could not compete any more. The original 6d fare had quickly been reduced to 1d for the journey from Whitburn to Seaside Lane. To put this into context, the miners strike had been seeking a guaranteed wage of five shillings (60d) per day for working at the coal face, and many men worked a six-day week for less than 20 shillings.

Success

Such was the success of the new service that in 1927 the partners gave up their original route from Stanley to concentrate on the Whitburn operation. Only one other route was ever operated, this running from Whitburn, through East and West Boldon to Boldon Colliery. It was taken over from George Puncheon in 1927 and operated as a summer service. Puncheon had been the only serious competitor to Economic; he and his driver (and nephew) George Weston spent their next 40 years working for Wilson. The Boldon Colliery route was seen as purely a leisure service, at its maximum it ran on only four days a week, including bank holidays.

The lock-out at Whitburn Colliery ended in December 1926, and at about the same time as the pit reopened the owners realigned their railway lines. The quarries were also extended with the result that the old toll road was closed. A new road nearer to the colliery was built to replace it, which was certainly wider and rather less steep. On their journeys to and from Whitburn the Economic buses now ran to a piece of vacant ground near the colliery (where the Co-op store was built in later years), then doubled back to return to the new connecting road. This situation did not last long, because during this period the highway authorities had been building a completely new road northwards along the coast, from the end of the old road at Souter Point, passing Marsden Grotto and Marsden Bay, all the way to the Pier Head at South Shields.

When this new road was ceremonially opened in November 1929, one of the first vehicles to use it was an Economic bus. Economic was now able to run its buses in a circular route around South Shields, alternate vehicles going clockwise via the 'High Road' and anti-clockwise along the new Coast Road. Clockwise buses took their layover at their old terminus in Ocean Road, while buses in the opposite direction usually only waited long enough to unload and load their passengers at the town end of Fowler Street before resuming their journey. The new road also had the advantage of removing the need for the awkward 'double-back' arrangement at Whitburn Colliery.

To maintain these services both partners bought new buses. In 1926 Anderson bought a 20-seat Reo Major, with a locally built body, and a 26-seater Leyland. The latter was to lead to a long association with Leyland, though he also bought a Hall Lewis-bodied Dennis at the same time. His next buses were a pair of Leyland-bodied Lioness PLC1s and a couple of Leyland Lion LTs; the last two survived World War 2. Wilson chose various models of Reo, buying seven, and in 1928 a Gilford 166 was acquired. Neither of the partners was averse to buying the occasional used vehicle, and a few real bargains were obtained from time to time. For example, when the 1930 Road Traffic Act came into effect, several operators either lost their licences or went out of business. Wilson obtained his first Albions in this way.

At the other end of the route, Sunderland Corporation began its own motorbus services in 1928. One proposed service would have reached Whitburn, but this never materialised. For its part, Economic applied to the Sunderland police, who were responsible for granting road-service licences in that town, for permission to operate into the town centre. This was refused, so Economic appealed to the Ministry of Transport against the decision. The company went ahead in the meantime by extending the service by about a mile to an off-road private parking ground in Roker. This was of great value to the company, as it was near to the Sunderland AFC ground, which naturally generated much traffic.

Useful connections

The Ministry of Transport granted the Economic appeal, and even improved on its application by stipulating that the terminus should be at Park Lane. This gave useful connections for those travellers who wished to continue their journeys by bus, as Park Lane had become the main Sunderland terminus for Northern General, Sunderland District and several other company bus services. The new route went along the main shopping street and had bus stops at both Sunderland and Monkwearmouth railway stations, giving further useful connections.

Operation of this extension did not however begin at once. A new Wearmouth Bridge was in course of construction over the river Wear around the structure of the old bridge. This was causing a lot of congestion, and the various bus operators were asked to co-operate in trying to reduce this. Economic therefore refrained from beginning its new service until the new bridge was completed and officially opened in October 1929. There was one drawback: the Ministry of Transport had attempted to give the Sunderland trams some protection from the interloper by routeing the buses on to roads away from the tram route between Roker and the new bridge. This meant that the Economic buses went along some extremely poorly-surfaced and steeply-cambered roads through a very old residential area. When some years later it was suggested that Economic should adopt double-deck buses, the state of these roads was cited as the reason against doing this.

Sunderland Corporation announced that there had been an immediate drop in receipts on its trams as a direct result of the new Economic service. It then put work in hand to improve its Sea Lane terminus by laying extra sidings and a turning loop. These facilities were opened in 1931 and enabled the trams to turn around much more quickly when crowds cascaded on to the beaches on fine summer days. A better service was then achieved with fewer trams, and the new terminus was re-named Seaburn.

Autonomous businesses

Until now Economic had operated as a full partnership sharing all costs and receipts. As is often the case with self-made men, Anderson and Wilson frequently found themselves at loggerheads over points of principle, due to their differing styles of management. Consequently they agreed to separate their interests and to operate as two autonomous businesses with a shared fleetname. There was no change as far as the public was concerned, but for the former partners, it was 'to each his own', with individual bus fleets, crews, workshops, offices and even tickets; the conductors always accepted the return tickets of both operators, of course. The livery of both bus fleets remained maroon and cream, though even these shades varied slightly from time to time. All buses carried their owner's names in large letters on the back, and both fleets had their own numbering arrangements. In later years, Anderson painted his coaches maroon and coffee, and Wilson's coaches wore a reversed layout of the maroon and cream.

Anderson preferred block letters for the fleetname, while Wilson used script, though even here there were exceptions. Anderson's garage was at The Bents, on the coast road at the southern end of Whitburn, and Wilson kept his buses at Roker, near the north

Anderson's no.1 was one of a pair of Crossley-bodied Leyland Tiger Cubs built in 1957.
R L Kell

Sunderland docks. He later moved to larger premises in Southwick Road, quite close to the Sunderland Corporation main tram depot and offices. Anderson's legal address was 'The Bents Garage', where his office was situated, while Wilson had an office in Adolphus Street, Whitburn, which was his legal address.

Next, Sunderland Corporation attempted to buy out the Economic. A meeting was held in 1932 where by all accounts a 'fly on the wall' would have died laughing. Apparently the meeting dissolved into a full-blown argument between Anderson and Wilson, each of whom tried to buy the other out! Needless to say, Sunderland withdrew from the discussions, presumably in the hope that the pair would finally fall out completely and the business fail. In fact, Economic survived the end of Sunderland Corporation Transport by nine months!

Shared

Between 1930 and 1940 Anderson shared his orders for new buses between Leyland and Dennis. The Leylands were an LT5 and an LT5A, both with Burlingham bus bodies, and two LT7s with diesel engines and Leyland bodies. Three Dennis Lancets, all with Dennis coach bodies, completed the prewar fleet. Wilson, on the other hand, became a staunch Albion supporter with no fewer than nine, of which

two carried coach bodies; there were also two Leyland Lion LT7s, which had locally-built bodies by Blagg of Sunderland. Wilson also added a second-hand Gilford to his fleet in 1935, but disposed of it after two years. At one time South Shields Corporation had fewer buses than Wilson!

Meanwhile, a new trolleybus service was being implemented by South Shields Corporation in 1936 between the town centre and the district known as Cleadon Park, which should not be confused with Cleadon (village), situated two miles further south. The route replaced that of an existing motor-bus service, and our interest in it concerns its extension eastwards to the new Coast Road at Marsden Bay in 1937. The opening of this extension coincided with a visit by the Prince of Wales, who travelled along the Coast Road, and consequently both the Economic service and the new trolleybus service were very heavily loaded on that occasion.

South Shields Corporation also took the next step; a new trolleybus route was constructed between the southern town boundary at Marsden Grotto and the town centre via the Coast Road. It is doubtful whether this route ever made any profit, because there were few domestic or employment objectives along the Coast Road, so that it really only served the beaches, cafés and public houses. Economic, on the other hand, continued to carry useful loads of passengers over the same road, carrying them to and from their homes in Whitburn. The trolleybuses only came into their own on fine sunny summer days, but this being the North Sea coast . . .

War

Little immediate effect was felt by Economic when war started in 1939, but early in 1940 the Coast Road was closed by the military between Souter Point and the Pier Head at South Shields. Miles of barbed wire ensured that invading forces would have difficulty in making a landing from the sea. It also deterred small boys from trying to sneak on to the beaches for a forbidden swim!

The Economic service was then forced to use Lizard Lane for all journeys into South Shields. From the town terminus they then proceeded east along Ocean Road before turning south up Woodbine Street and followed several other twists and turns through the town before re-emerging on to the existing route near Horsley Hill. This enforced diversion was of course followed in both directions, thus retaining the two-way circular South Shields loops.

In Sunderland a similar inland route had to be used by Economic during the war years due to the closure of the road between Seaburn and Roker. The difference here was that while the heavily-used tram service was suspended, a compensatory corporation bus service through Fulwell was needed, whereas the closing of the South Shields trolleybus route probably saved money.

The Economic bus fleets survived the war unscathed, the only losses being of Anderson's Leyland LT5 no.L6 (UP 8062) and Wilson's oldest bus, Albion no.1 (TY 3761) which were requisitioned by the War Office in 1940, never to be seen again. Both depots suffered slight damage during the very severe air raids between 1940 and 1942. Many route diversions were necessary in both South Shields and Sunderland, there being great damage done to both towns, with heavy loss of life, many injured people and buildings reduced to rubble. Nor did the weather help, heavy snow falling during the winter of 1940/1 which closed many roads for weeks. One Economic bus was marooned in a snowdrift in Lizard Lane for about ten days, and the services could not operate for some time.

Reopened

With the Allied forces on the offensive in mainland Europe in 1944, it was felt by the authorities that the threat of invasion was over, and in mid-1944 the

Coast Road in South Shields and Whitburn Road at Roker were reopened to traffic. Economic services resumed their prewar routes and the leisure-starved public flocked to the seaside, giving the Economic some of their best-ever passenger figures. The timetable required buses to leave Park Lane every 20 minutes, giving one bus every 40 minutes in each direction round the South Shields loop. For this three buses from each operator were needed but traffic was so intense, particularly at weekends, that as many as six more buses would be run as duplicates. Even then standing loads were normal.

Like most operators at the end of the war, both Anderson and Wilson found that their buses were worn-out and living on borrowed time. The first postwar delivery was of a pair of Albion CX13 buses at the end of 1945. These carried semi-utility Pickering bodies and went into the Wilson fleet. Anderson had to buy a second-hand Duple-bodied Guy Arab coach in 1947 while waiting for two new Guy Arabs with Associated Coachbuilders (ACB) bodywork. ACB was the new name for the Blagg company of Sunderland, which had built a number of bodies for Economic before the war. The three Guys were the only Gardner-engined vehicles to be owned by either operator. Wilson went on to buy a number of Albions, both new and second-hand, until 1954. Anderson, on the other hand, standardised on Leyland chassis until 1957. In addition, Wilson sent two prewar Albions and a Leyland Lion to ACB where new bodies were built for them.

Interestingly both Anderson and Wilson always took a mixture of bus and coach bodies. Though they regarded bus operation as their business, and never became involved in coach operation, they nevertheless realised that there was a lucrative private-hire market for day and evening trips to football matches, social clubs and so forth. Hence the need was there for vehicles suitable for both bus and coach use.

Poor results

The Boldon-Whitburn service was reinstated in 1947, having been withdrawn during the war years. The results were poor, made worse the following year by the introduction of a new Northern General service. This ran hourly from Newcastle to Cleadon, then by a parallel route to that of Economic to Whitburn and finally along the coast to terminate at Seaburn. At first the Economic tried to retaliate with an increased service, but quickly reverted to weekend and bank-holiday journeys only. With a restricted number of journeys, the route was little used and was withdrawn in the early 1960s.

By contrast, the main Sunderland-South Shields route was carrying so many passengers that an application was made to the Traffic Commissioners to allow an increased service. This was granted in 1947, a 15-minute frequency was now operated, with

Mounting a Plaxton coach body on an Albion Aberdonian chassis produced a very rare combination. This was no.4 of 1958 in the Anderson fleet.
R L Kell

buses in alternate directions around the South Shields loop as before. On Saturdays, and on summer afternoons and evenings, the frequency was increased to 10 minutes. Six buses were required for the 15-minute service, and the 10-minute frequency needed eight.

An equal number of duties was operated by each partner, departing consecutively in sets of three or four, according to the timetable requirements. These duties were alternated every day so that over a period of 14 days each partner achieved equal mileage and duties. Large numbers of duplicates were required on sunny weekends. These were usually operated between Sunderland and Whitburn, though when Sunderland Football Club played at home the duplicates came to Roker Park from South Shields and Whitburn. Each partner was responsible for duplicating his own duties.

In 1945 South Shields Corporation had announced a scheme to construct trolleybus routes over nearly all the main roads in the town, including the Westoe-Harton-Horsley Hill portion of the Economic route. Because of the delay in obtaining overhead equipment and vehicles, a motor-bus service was started as an interim measure. Significantly, waiting passengers would ignore the blue South Shields

buses, preferring to wait for the Economic buses, which had served them loyally for two decades. Eventually the South Shields service was reduced to three daily journeys, and the trolleybus project for that route was abandoned. Meanwhile, many sections of trolleybus route did get built, including one between Horsley Hill and Marsden Inn. This was part of a long circular service and had little if any effect on Economic passenger levels.

Replaced

The majority of the older buses in the Economic fleets were replaced between the end of the war and 1950. Anderson bought nine: the three Guys already mentioned and six Leyland Tiger PS1s and PS2s. Wilson took seven during the same period, all Albion Valkyrie CX13 and Valiant CX19 models. Between then and 1956 the only additional vehicle was a second-hand Albion CX13 coach, which was bought by Wilson in 1954.

The last prewar survivors in the Anderson fleet were sold to a showman in 1954. These two Leyland Lion LT7As with Leyland all-metal bodies, probably the last of their type in service, would have been prime candidates for the preservation movement had it existed then. Wilson tended to keep his vehicles rather longer. His last prewar Albion remained in the fleet until 1957, and the last rebodied example was not retired until 1962.

Meanwhile the National Coal Board, successor to the Harton Coal Company, was busy modernising its railway. Most of the steam engines were replaced by diesels, but the old carriages were so dilapidated, and carried so few passengers, that it was decided to withdraw them entirely in 1953, the line to Whitburn being retained for coal traffic only. In November buses replaced the passenger trains, two services to Whitburn Colliery being operated at shift times. Service 'A' ran from South Shields (Mile End Road) via Westoe and Service 'B' ran from South Shields (Market) via Tyne Dock. Some journeys were operated as Service 'C', an amalgam of the two. The Traffic Commissioners granted Economic, Northern General and South Shields Corporation equal running powers in these new services, which were subsidised by the Coal Board. The Economic found itself unable to contribute its share of the operation and allowed Northern General to work its journeys. Northern paid Economic 1d (1/2p) for each mile operated. Like many rail-replacement services, they were little used and were withdrawn in 1968. A bus station was built at Whitburn Colliery for these buses and the main services also called there. More importantly, Wilson built a new garage adjacent to this facility, opened in 1953, though he retained his workshop at Southwick Road and offices at Adolphus Street.

Economic bus-stop signs were conspicuous by their absence. Regular passengers knew where to wait, and most stops were eventually shared by other operators who fixed their own signs. A few signs could be found in South Shields that had been erected by the council, but when that authority asked for payment from Economic, it was ignored.

Fleet renewal re-started in 1956 when Wilson became the owner of the first underfloor-engined Economic vehicle. An AEC Reliance, it was the forerunner of ten bought between that year and 1963, one of which was bodied as a coach, and one other seated as a dual-purpose vehicle, the remainder being buses. All had Roe bodies with the exception of the first, fitted with a Duple (Midland) body, and the final pair, bodied by Plaxton.

In the following year, Anderson bought two Leyland Tiger Cubs with the unusual choice of Crossley bus bodies and one Burlingham-bodied AEC Reliance. Crossley was famous for its bus bodies, but only six of this particular style of single-decker were built, the other four going to Stockport Corporation. They were amongst the last bodies

to be built by Crossley before its closure. One further Tiger Cub and a solitary Albion Aberdonian arrived in 1958; the latter could best be described as a lightweight Tiger Cub. Obviously pleased by the Reliance, in the period from 1959 to 1967 Anderson acquired eight more, of which two were coaches; these all carried Plaxton bodywork.

Strike

As was to be expected in an area dominated by heavy industry, the employees of Economic were all members of a union, in their case the Municipal & General Workers' Union. There was little militancy however, and it was not until 1957 that the first strike occurred. This was in support of a national bus strike, but the M&GWU quickly informed them that the argument was with the large operators and not really their concern, so they returned to work.

In 1964 the last front-engined vehicles were withdrawn. This meant that it would have been possible to convert the service to one-person operation. Anderson and Wilson were unwilling to do this; they believed that the personal service given to passengers by conductors justified their need. They also realised that it would mean increased journey times, requiring additional buses. Finally, Economic was still using pre-printed bus tickets punched by the conductors; the purchase (or lease) of ticket machines and the work involved in fitting them to the buses was felt to be an unnecessary expense. So the khaki-coated conductors, hats at rakish angles, helping with pushchairs, parcels and passengers, continued to be a feature of Economic operation.

Tickets

The conductors' ticket racks were quite large, with two rows of tickets on each side. They carried 16 different-value 'Bell Punch' style single tickets, as well as 13 returns, an exchange ticket and a 12-journey ticket. The latter was a useful device, of multiple value for different pre-determined regular journeys. It incorporated a duplicate copy retained by the conductor, to be handed in with his daily takings. The single tickets were all coloured differently: returns were white, overprinted with the value in different colours, exchanges were orange and the multi-journey tickets were green and white. Tickets were validated by Bell Punches in the early days of the Economic. These were replaced by strap-mounted nippers, but latterly hand-held punches, suspended from the cash bag by a long chain, were the order of the day.

Economic needed a platform staff of 36 to maintain the services, and in addition each proprietor employed his own fitters, cleaners and an inspector. Tickets on both owners' buses were checked by whichever inspector was on duty. Most of the clerical duties were carried out with a staff of three in Anderson's office, to avoid duplication.

Wilson made a financial contribution towards this.

In 1969 the Economic drivers and conductors realised that though they were paid the full union rates for the job, but all other bus crews in the area received more money because they were awarded a bonus for one-person operation. The Economic platform staff thus decided to approve one-person operation so that they would qualify for the bonus. They told the owners, who refused to consider this, and a six-week strike followed. An appeal to arbitration supported the owners and the disgruntled employees returned to work with no more money in their pay packets and six weeks' debts to pay off.

The beginning of the end

To use an old cliché, this was the beginning of the end for Economic. Passenger numbers had declined since the peak of 1.8 million in 1952, though not as steeply as in the bus industry generally. Nevertheless the owners were finding it difficult to finance the purchase of new buses, since they lacked the bargaining power of the larger operators. Not only that; the underfloor-engined buses were costing more to maintain, and their lives were disappointingly short. The first Tiger Cub was withdrawn when only seven years old, the same year as the last front-engined Tiger left the fleet, at twice that age.

The final vehicle purchase by Wilson was of two Bedford VAL twin-steering coaches with Duple bodies, delivered in 1964 and 1965. As these were not very suitable for stage-carriage work they were mainly used for private hire, and this appears to have been a last attempt to find increased revenue. Anderson managed a few later purchases, including the final three of the previously mentioned Reliances in 1965-7. A second-hand Leyland Tiger Cub was bought in 1971, and his last new buses comprised a Bedford YRT and a YRQ, which arrived in 1973, with Plaxton and Willowbrook bus bodies respectively. Unfortunately, when only a few months old, the Bedford YRQ was involved in an accident which reduced the vehicle to scrap. It was replaced by a similar vehicle, which was exhibited at the Commercial Motor Show at Earls Court in 1974 before delivery to Economic.

The biggest threat to the existence of the company came in 1969 with the establishment of the Tyneside Passenger Transport Executive. One of the main tasks of the executive was to integrate all local transport in the area. South Shields Corporation buses were taken over immediately. Sunderland followed in 1973, after which the executive became the Tyne & Wear PTE. The PTE allocated new route numbers to its bus services and those of Northern General, and timetables were significantly altered. The Northern vehicles were also painted in a version of the PTE livery, so that the maroon Economic buses found themselves isolated in a sea of yellow buses. This was

Later Plaxton bus bodies had BET-style windscreens, as with 1975 AEC Reliance no.17, in the Anderson fleet, here alongside no.5, also from the Anderson fleet, a 1958 Leyland Tiger Cub/Plaxton. R L Kell

the last straw, the Economic operation with its single route was no longer a viable proposition in these circumstances. There was only one decision left to make: to which operator should Economic be sold – Northern General or Tyne & Wear PTE?

On 1 January 1975 the 22 remaining Economic buses and their service came under the ownership of the Tyne & Wear PTE. There were 10 Anderson vehicles, two of which had already been withdrawn and were non-runners. Of the 12 buses acquired from Wilson, one was in use as a static store and canteen, and two others had been unlicensed for some time. George Anderson took a well-earned retirement, and Teddy Wilson's son Archie, who had taken over the running of the business from his father, recounted enjoying his first night of uninterrupted sleep for years.

As far as the general public was concerned, the end came gradually; the only immediate change was to the legal ownership details on the sides of the buses. The Economic garages were closed, and the vehicles and crews worked from the South Shields depot in Dean Road. To cover for vehicle failures, former Sunderland Corporation Leyland Panthers with their distinctive Strachans bodies were used, crewed as usual by former Economic drivers and conductors.

On Sunday 23 March 1975 it was all over. A fleet of ten new Leyland Nationals took to the road in full PTE colours with ticket machines and without conductors. The PTE replaced the Economic services with a mixture of old and new links, rationalising existing town services in Sunderland and South Shields at the same time. The route from Sunderland began at the new Central Bus Station and, in addition to the existing route through Roker,

alternate buses ran along Newcastle Road to Fulwell before reaching Whitburn Road at Seaburn. In South Shields the Coast Road service continued unchanged but terminated at the Market, in common with most other South Shields routes. The 'High Road' service was diverted at Westoe to serve Chichester and Laygate before reaching the Market. Thus the town circular was maintained, but the extended circuitous 'High Road' service was less useful to Whitburn residents wishing to reach the shops in Fowler Street and King Street.

The South Shields PTE depot still operated a number of former South Shields Corporation rear-entrance double-deckers, so that there was employment available for the Economic conductors, and the drivers and fitters were offered jobs at either South Shields or Sunderland.

PTE livery

The buses were not so fortunate, only two receiving PTE livery and fleetnumbers. These were Anderson's Bedford YRT and YRQ, both of which had been less than a year old. They were transferred to the Armstrong-Galley subsidiary fleet, and were sold in 1977. All the other vehicles were sold to a dealer.

While this is strictly the end of the story of Economic, two interesting points are worth making. In 1980 the whole fleet of Leyland Nationals which had been bought to operate the service was sold to Burnley & Pendle Transport. From that time,

Restored to full working order by Alan Purvis, Wilson's 1949 Albion CX39 with ACB body, no.7, was in pristine condition when it arrived in Harrogate at the end of the 1988 Trans-Pennine run.
G Burrows

Whitburn was served with double-deck Leyland Atlantean buses with 86-seat Alexander bodies from the standard PTE allocation at South Shields.

A PTE initiative in 1985 was the reintroduction of some of the names and liveries of earlier days. Thus a batch of Atlanteans at South Shields was repainted into a double-deck version of the Economic colours, complete with authentic-style fleetnames. Some single-deckers also received Economic livery. The Lizard Lane-Harton-South Shields service was reinstated, the Laygate version was reduced in frequency and all three services were given distinctive route numbers, E1, E2 and E3. Inevitably, some of the Economic-liveried buses strayed on to South Shields town services occasionally.

George Anderson and Teddy Wilson would no doubt have found wry amusement in the thought that from their early endeavours, the Economic name and colours would become a familiar sight on buses seen in all parts of South Shields 60 years later.

Not only has the Economic Bus Service passed into history; so has Whitburn Colliery and the pit village around it. The colliery closed in 1968 and the site has been cleared; all that remains to be seen is the Souter lighthouse and the keeper's cottages, now preserved as a tourist attraction. Whitburn village has thankfully survived, a quiet haven in a world of change.

This account of the Economic Bus Service would not be complete without reference to the fine work achieved by the late Allan Purvis. He spent many years recording not only much data about the operator, but he went on to save five former Economic buses from the scrapheap. One of these was Albion Valiant CX39 no.7 (HUP 236), which was new in the Wilson fleet in 1947. Allan bought it after it had been withdrawn in 1964, and much time and money went into the painstaking restoration. This has one of two Associated Coachbuilders bodies known still to exist. The Albion is regularly shown at vehicle rallies around the North of England by Allan's brother John, and is a fitting memorial to Allan and to two dedicated busmen – George Anderson and Edward Wilson. **CB**

Acknowledgements

This article would not have been possible without the help and encouragement given to the author by Sybil Reeder of the Whitburn Local History Society, Val Craggs of Sunderland City Library & Arts Centre, and the staff of South Tyneside Leisure Services at the South Shields Central Library. My thanks go also to

Bob Davis, Bill Hatcher, Bob Kell, Roy Marshall, John Purvis, David Wayman, the PSV Circle and the Omnibus Society, and those who have kindly lent photographs. I have also used references to Economic from numerous books and magazines. Any errors or inaccuracies are of course those of the author.

ECONOMIC FLEETLISTS

ANDERSON

Fleet	Reg	Chassis/No.	Body	In/out
	J 5712	Siddeley-Deesy	Conversion B12R	1925
	CN 5427	Reo Major	Crescent	1926
	PT 4273	Leyland	Young	1926
	TN 3085	Dennis 31345	Hall Lewis B20F	1926
1	UP 1090	Leyland PLC1 46920	Leyland B26F	1928-35
2	TY 2218	Leyland PLC1 45437	Leyland B26F	1928-35
L3	UP 3433	Leyland LT1 50302	Leyland B32F	1929-47
L4	UP 5356	Leyland LT2 51556	Leyland B32F	1931-46
D5	UP 7045	Dennis Lancet 170195	Dennis C32F	1932-50
L6	UP 8062	Leyland LT5 3109	Burlingham B36F	1933-40
L7	UP 9206	Leyland LT5A 4511	Burlingham B37F	1934-46
D8	APT 792	Dennis Lancet 170967	Dennis C32F	1935-50
L9	AUP 361	Leyland LT7 10131	Leyland B36F	1936-54
D10	DPT 448	Dennis Lancet 2 175608	Dennis C35F	1938-
L11	APT 783	Leyland LT7 6419	Leyland B36F	1939-54
12	EF 7667	Guy Arab 5LW FD29183	Duple C35F	1947-59
13	GUP 389	Guy Arab 5LW FD29244	ACB B35F	1947-57
14	GUP 390	Guy Arab 5LW FD29246	ACB B35F	1947-57
15	HUP 28	Leyland PS1 462144	Duple C35F	1960-
16	HUP 29	Leyland PS1 462370	Duple C35F	1960-
17	KUP 759	Leyland PS1 496168	ACB B35F	1950-63
18	KUP 760	Leyland PS1 494350	ACB B35F	1950-61
19	LPT 176	Leyland PS2 496559	ACB B35F	1950-63
20	LPT 177	Leyland PS2 496560	ACB B35F	1950-64
1	VUP 327	Leyland PSUC 553578	Crossley B44F	1957-64
2	VUP 328	Leyland PSUC 553579	Crossley B44F	1957-65
3	VUP 329	AEC Reliance MU3RAE1290	Burlingham B45F	1957-67
4	638 APT	Albion MRN11N 82514C	Plaxton C41F	1958-66
5	639 APT	Leyland Reliance 586351	Plaxton B45F	1958-71
6	626 FPT	AEC Reliance 2MU3RV2430	Plaxton B45F	1959-67*
7	1106 PT	AEC Reliance 2MU3RV3087	Plaxton B45F	1960-67*
8	8231 PT	AEC Reliance 2MU3RA4187	Plaxton B55F	1962-8
9	6748 UP	AEC Reliance 4MU3RA4757	Plaxton B55F	1963-75*
12	CPT 389B	AEC Reliance 2MU3RA5373	Plaxton B55F	1964-75*
13	HPT 664C	AEC Reliance 2MU3RA5816	Plaxton C43F	1965-75*
14	OUP 325D	AEC Reliance 2MU3RA6499	Plaxton C43F	1966-75*
17	UPT 776E	AEC Reliance 6MU3R6650	Plaxton B55F	1967-75*
15	CPT 5B	Leyland PSUC L30584	Plaxton B47F	1971-5*
16	OPT 311M	Bedford YRQ CW455843	W'brook B47F	1973-4
18	TUP 161M	Bedford YRT DW454295	Plaxton B53F	1974-7
16	GGR 344N	Bedford YRQ DW456870	W'brook B47F	1974-7

Notes

J 5712 was new in 1919; PT 4273 was new in 1924; TY 2218 was new in 1926; APT 783 was new in 1935; EF 7667 was new in 1946; CPT 5B was new in 1964.

Vehicles marked * were all taken over by Tyne & Wear PTE and sold by April 1975.

OPT 311M was sold for scrap after accident.

TUP 161M and GGR 344N became Tyne & Wear PTE nos.41 and 844.

GGR 344N replaced no.16 (OPT 311M); it was shown at Earls Court 1974, as OPT 311N.

WILSON

Fleet	Reg	Chassis/No.	Body	In/out
	PT 4359	Reo Speedwagon	B14F	1924
	PT 4038	Reo Speedwagon	C14F	1925
	PT 6391	Reo Major	B20F	1925
	PT 9001	Reo Major	B20F	1927
	PT 9062	Reo Sprinter G5701	B20F	1927
	CN 3722	Reo Sprinter FAX6400	B20F	1928-33
	CN 3766	Gilford 166D	B26R	1928
	CN 2438	Reo TG73823		1930
1	TY 3761	Albion PM28 7016A	B32F	1930-9
2	TY 3762	Albion PM28 7017C	B32F	1930-6
3	UA 2326	Albion PM28 7018A	B20F	1930
4	UP 6326	Albion PW65 16009H	Alexander B32F	1931-48
5	UP 7988	Albion PW65 16027C	Alexander B32F	1933-49
6	UP 9341	Albion PW67 16204B	NCME B32F	1934-49
7	CN 4317	Gilford 1660T 11187	? B32F	1935-7
8	AUP 24	Leyland LT7 10489	Blagg B36F	1936-55
9	BUP 569	Leyland LT7 12904	Blagg B38F	1937-56
10	DPT 124	Albion PK114 25019C	Blagg C32F	1938-55
11	DUP 853	Albion CX19 58013J	Blagg C39F	1939-57
12	EPT 107	Albion CX13 58016C	Blagg B32F	1939-62
1	FUP 367	Albion CX13 58024A	Pickering B32F	1945-60
2	FUP 368	Albion CX13 58024B	Pickering B32F	1945-60
3	FUP 786	Albion CX13 58029E	ACB B35F	1946-58
6	HUP 235	Albion CX39 60303C	ACB C33F	1949-62
7	HUP 236	Albion CX39 60303D	ACB C33F	1949-64
4	HUP 739	Albion CX13 58056L	ACB C33F	1948-58
10	KUP 799	Albion CX39 60311B	ACB C33F	1950-63
12	HUP 159	Albion CX13 58049B	Beccols C33F	1954-7
11	UPT 630	AEC Reliance MU3RV539	Duple B44F	1956-72*
8	VUP 472	AEC Reliance MU3RV1179	Roe B44F	1957-75*
9	VUP 473	AEC Reliance MU3RV1180	Roe B44F	1957-74*
12	YPT 795	AEC Reliance MU3RV1557	Roe B44F	1958-75*
3	YPT 796	AEC Reliance MU3RV1559	Roe C41C	1958-75*
1	901 FUP	AEC Reliance 2MU3RV2869	Roe B44F	1960-73*
2	902 FUP	AEC Reliance 2MU3RV2870	Roe B44F	1960-75*
4	2372 PT	AEC Reliance 2MU3RV3698	Roe DP41F	1961-75*
7	8031 PT	AEC Reliance 4MU3RA4138	Plaxton B55F	1962-75*
8	6623 PT	AEC Reliance 4MU3RA4756	Plaxton B55F	1963-75*
7	535 MUP	Bedford VAL14 1411	Duple C52F	1964-75*
10	FPT 440C	Bedford VAL14 1533	Duple C52F	1965-75*

Notes

PT 4038 was new in 1924; CN 2438 was new in 1925; TY 3761/2 were new in 1927; UA 2326 was new in 1928; CN 4317 was new in 1930.

AUP 24 and BUP 569 were rebodied B35F by ACB in 1947.

EPT 107 was rebodied C33F by ACB in 1950 and renumbered 5.

Vehicles marked * were all taken over by Tyne & Wear PTE and sold by April 1975.

HUP 236 is restored and preserved.

Born: Lowestoft, Suffolk 1 July 1936
Parents: Tilling & British Automobile Traction, which set up a new company to take over what had begun life as the bodybuilding division of United Automobile Services and, since 1931, had been part of the new Eastern Counties Omnibus Company.
How did all that come about?: Although United was best known as the territorial operator covering much of North East England, it started out in

CHECK POINT

No.3:
Eastern Coach Works

Lowestoft in 1912 and was building bus bodies in the town from 1919, for its own and other operators' use. Consolidation and growth of the bus industry led Tilling & BAT, which acquired control of United in 1929, to restructure its East Anglian interests in 1931. Hence the creation of ECOC.
So why then set up ECW?: Tilling, which dominated the short-lived T&BAT group, was becoming more self-sufficient, especially following its acquisition of Bristol Tramways in 1931, and the Lowestoft factory was also winning custom from more operators outside the group. So it made sense to set this up as more of a free-standing business, building largely on Bristol chassis. But T&BAT actually came close to selling the factory in 1933.
To whom?: In their excellent Venture Transport history of ECW, Maurice Doggett and Alan Townsin discovered that Charles Roberts, the Wakefield bodybuilder, negotiated to buy the factory, but pulled out of the possible deal. Roberts was a railway wagon maker, but it also bodied buses and trams into the early post-World War 2 period. It might still have been in the market today had it bought what later became ECW. And the Lowestoft plant might have remained in existence, too.
But the creation of ECW led to a long period of uninterrupted production?: A long period of production, but hardly uninterrupted. The import of a new management team, notably a manager from Charles H Roe in Leeds, helped gear things up for the rest of the 1930s, but big trouble loomed on 28 May 1940.
What happened then?: What happened was because of the fear of something that mercifully didn't happen. Amid great, real fear of a Nazi invasion in the wake of the fall of France and the Low Countries, the factory was evacuated and such production as could be salvaged was moved into emergency accommodation in a United Counties garage at Irthlingborough, Northamptonshire. Although production returned to bomb-damaged Lowestoft in

January 1945, Irthlingborough was kept going for another seven years.
So Irthlingborough built utility bodies?: Strictly speaking, yes, but they were a lot less utilitarian in appearance than those from most other British bus factories. This was partly because most were rebodied prewar chassis and it seems that the Ministry of Supply was less fussed about design standards on them, but even when new Bristol Ks started coming out of the plant in 1943, they had rounded window mountings that gave a very clear idea of what ECW's postwar bodies would be like for the best part of the next 40 years. In a sense, you could almost argue that postwar ECW bodies were derived from a utility design.
What happened to its postwar market?: It changed dramatically in 1948 when Tilling sold out to the new state-owned British Transport Commission. BTC ownership forbade ECW and Bristol from supplying the private, municipal or export markets, so it could no longer supply BET, independents or corporations. Not even Lowestoft Corporation, on its doorstep. But it compensated for their loss by supplying other bits of BTC, like the Scottish Bus Group, London Transport and the bit of the Sheffield fleet that was owned by British Railways. And it was during this period that it perhaps had its finest hours.
Doing what?: Building all of the bodies on the revolutionary Bristol Lodekka, Britain's first successful lowheight double-decker.
How did it get back into the open market?: In 1965 Leyland bought a 25% shareholding that was increased to 50% in 1969. This brought several municipal operators in particular into the fold. But it may ultimately have led to the company's demise.
Why was that?: Bus demand plummeted after 1980, when the new bus grant scheme began to be phased out, then the National Bus Company sold its 50% interest in ECW, Bristol and Leyland National in 1982. Leyland was steadily closing bus plants: Park Royal shut in 1979, Bristol in 1982, Roe in 1984. ECW closed in 1987, after completing 260 Leyland Olympians for London Buses.
Its most unusual products?: Despite building huge numbers of standard products, there were many over the years. These included KSW-style bodies on tin-front Leyland PD2s for Sheffield, London Transport's prototype Green Line Routemaster and the GS class of Guy midibuses and it finished a Danish-built Leyland DAB Tiger Cub that might have been the first of many had circumstances been different.
If the Lodekka was its finest hour, what was its worst?: Almost certainly the B51, a 1981/2 coach body on Leyland Leopards and Tigers for NBC. Structural problems beset these vehicles and took something away from the company's largely untarnished reputation.

Alan Millar

A typical ECW body of the 1970s, but mounted, unusually, on Ford R1014 chassis. Fifty were built in 1973 for NBC – 25 for Hants & Dorset and 25 for Alder Valley, as seen on the latter's no.714 in Guildford in January 1978.
Michael Dryhurst

THE LAST THING ON MY MIND

In what he chooses to deem one of the wildest places on earth, ROBERT E JOWITT – perhaps more than usually obsessively eccentric on some 'off-the-road' attractions, yet not without the expected comments on 'the fair sex' – manages in his forays into South Wales to throw in a bus here and there . . .

True love and trolleybus, Sweetheart and single-decker. Oh, how cruel the fate that tore us apart!
It was sad that the Cardiff BUT 9641T/East Lancs trolleybuses were scrapped, too . . .
All photos taken by Robert E Jowitt between 1961 and 1964, except where otherwise noted

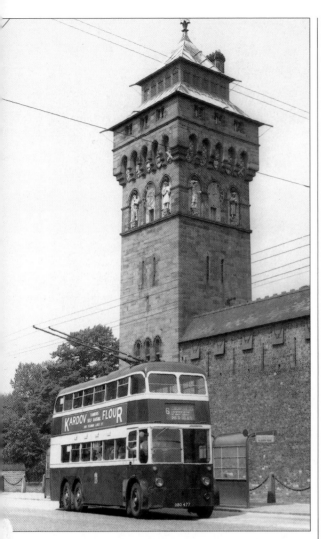

The second Marquis of Bute changed Cardiff from a village of 2,000 souls to the greatest coal-shipping port of the Victorian era; his son coupled his whims with the talents of the architect William Burges to add a Welsh-French-Gothic castle. It formed a fine backdrop for Cardiff trolleybuses like this 1948 BUT/East Lancs.

of us was a cottage with holes in the roof, which looked like shell damage.

By holding her hand, bidding her shut her eyes and put her feet where I told her, I led Sweetheart through the tiny space between the dead head and the brink of the raging stream. Before the cottage the hillside opened out a bit, and though there were several more corpses we were able to pass them easily enough, but their presence made her look elsewhere and with a scream she pointed to the eastern lip of the cup. Along the very edge of the precipice marched a long line of uniformed men in single file.

I looked round. Along the west side another file marched. Considering what the nature of the ground up there must be the men managed to maintain a remarkable degree of military precision in pace and spacing. As the storm blotted them from our sight we hid in the cottage.

Of the cottage's former occupants there was no trace save the chassis and wheels of a pram, dingy curtains in some of the windows, and a heap of letters and official forms, mostly in indecipherable tongue but one – apparently the first draft of a letter – in uncertain English explaining the owner's inability to maintain his position in the prevailing circumstances.

Forbidden territory

A glimpse through the gale revealed that the marching men had now disappeared, presumably into the – to us – forbidden territory south of the cwm, and as the rain had to some extent abated we set out again, henceforth ascending contours which on the map were so close together as to be almost solid, until at a twist where the path crossed a ledge running more or less level below the craggy tops of the cup I sighted – as I had hoped I might – a large square stone with two holes in it. 'We're on the track!' I cried in triumph, and we set out westwards – for I could see at once it was that way the object of my mission lay – along the ledge. It was probably a dozen feet broad, good enough for even a vertigo-sufferer like me, except where its outer side had crumbled away and where rock-falls from above had narrowed it, so we made good progress until we came to the horse.

People don't generally dwell on what the Charge of the Light Brigade looked like afterwards, but neither Sweetheart nor I were going to get past this one, it was revoltingly right across one of the narrower parts . . . but I was determined to reach the spot I sought so we retraced our steps until we found a horrid dripping gully up which we climbed with

N O, AT THAT MOMENT, buses were perhaps the last thing on my mind. My main pre-occupation was how to get Sweetheart past the corpse. In all my forays into these wild valleys I had other objects to attain or duties to perform, looking at buses not among them – or only incidentally – and here and now this very dead and mutilated body was barring our passage, stretched right across the narrow path – we had been compelled to abandon our transport half a mile back when the track became impossible – with an unscaleable rocky wall on the one hand and a roaring torrent below us on the other.

'I don't want to look at it,' Sweetheart said. 'We can't go on!'

We were just about on the 1,000ft contour, and on either side and ahead the mountain walls rose up, when not obscured by heavy squalls of rain which was only just not sleet, another 500ft like the rim of a cup . . . or rather half a cup. A little way ahead

Following practice (thoroughly foreign) employed on Cardiff trams of seated conductor and passenger flow, Cardiff trolleybuses started off with the same notion, very unusual on British trolleybuses and a habit later abandoned in Cardiff, but you can still see the out-of-use sliding door front exit on this 1948 BUT/East Lancs specimen.

Smoking chimneys of terraces on the valley floor, pigeon lofts and allotment gardens climbing above, and above again a rather choice but utterly unidentifiable bus straying along a lane . . . and, out of frame, probably as much mountainside as the area of the picture . . . which is taken at Six Bells, just south of Abertillery

Left: *Your average and not very noteworthy Red & White Bristol LS is about to rush under the spidery limbs of the Crumlin viaduct while a tank engine of GWR ilk snuffles on the low level. The diagonal scar up the opposite side of the valley looks as if it might have been of interest to this author but if it was he can no longer remember what it represented.*

Below: *When I tread the verge of Jordan . . . well, anyway, this picture is in Cwm Rhondda and the chap in the overalls appears to be treading into a fairly dangerous position relative to the Rhondda AEC Regent V/Weymann, while from the chapel on the left (see* **Classic Bus Yearbook 8**, *page 71, for further Jowitt elucidation on such buildings) with its gable echoed by the slag heaps on the mountain summits the strains of Cwm Rhondda must oft-times have resounded.*

A not-unpleasant if somewhat bottom-heavy-looking AEC Regent III/Bruce of Gelligaer UDC, somewhere up in the hills near Gelligaer by a thoroughly horrible bus shelter. The Ford Prefect framed therein is quite nice too, isn't it, and was actually the author's – or rather his father's – and played quite a part in South Welsh expeditions.

slimy rocks and spiky hawthorns for hand holds and me pulling her up with the sodden belt of my coat until we reached the point where earlier the file of men had marched, then we followed the rim until I judged we were well past the horse and found another gully, as noisome as the first, by which we returned down to the ledge . . . and carried on some way until I saw ahead the scene I had hoped for, unchanged from my illustration of 25 years before. And better still, as the accompanying text had promised but more than I had dared to hope, five pieces of the treasure lay scattered around. One bit, the best, intact, was far below the precipice, wedged against a hawthorn tree, inaccessible, but I doubt that even could we have reached it we could have carried it for the weight of the smaller broken pieces to hand proved dreadful enough. We cached two under rocks and earth, with the hope of returning sometime, and, struggling under the other two, set out back the way we had come.

Obviously we had to bypass the dead specimen of light cavalry again, and this time in those horrid gullies we were encumbered with precious heavy metal. I won't dwell on the difficulties and discomforts. When we reached the cottage once more we put them on the pram chassis which made their carriage far easier. Now there was only the hurdle of the first corpse – I led Sweetheart past it as before, then had to make three more traverses for the treasure and the pram – and at last we were back in weather which after the hell of the summits seemed almost spring-like . . .

No, it's not out of James Bond or John Buchan, and it's all absolutely true.

No, I hadn't come here to look at buses. This, the

Bryn Oer Tramroad, was what I came for. I do not believe that any of my regular bus readers, by now, expect me to write actually about buses (although, as, I hope, they know I can) but rather that I should write about the world in which the buses were. *And I must say that in all my visits to The Valleys, none of them inspired by bus hunting, I could not fail to see and admire the buses.* So yes, I came for the Bryn Oer Tramroad and its perilous course along the precipices of Duffryn Crawnon, maybe one of the bravest pieces of early railway construction in the world; the picture was from the *Railway Magazine* of April 1939 and had bewitched me for a decade (ever since my father bought in a load of second-hand RMs in Coronation year, 1953, or thereabouts . . . and before any London bus enthusiasts start getting the wrong idea let me say that our erudite editor and myself are in agreement that my late father was *not* a dealer in derelict Routemasters!), the marching men were probably Territorial Army or even boy scouts, the cottage had been abandoned because the man couldn't get his children to school, the corpses were raven-picked sheep and a mountain pony which must have slipped over the edge in a snowstorm, and the treasure was L-profile plate-rails.

Trolleybuses

So, no, it wasn't ever about buses. Once it was the death throes of the Swansea & Mumbles railway, even if the best and almost unique interurban tramways aren't allowed in the pages of *Classic Bus*, and of course once or twice I threw in the Cardiff trolleybuses – which must be allowed even if on my first session at them and especially those lovely single-deckers I blured about ten shots by having

Abergavenny bus station in midwinter rain boasts two choice motor cars and two fine buses . . . a Red & White AEC Regal III/Lydney, and the inevitable Western Welsh Tiger Cub.

photographed the corporation crest at 3ft range and forgotten to refocus to infinity – and once it was because a mate of mine at Bournemouth Art College wanted to go back to his birthplace and meet his old chums in Pontypridd (and use my car for the purpose) and more than once it was because Sweetheart had an elder sister in bungaloid respectability in Penarth. Sister and husband laid out a camp bed for me; 'A palliasse', said husband, and I whispered to Sweetheart: 'A palliasse laid out by a bally asse!'

And it was the Crumlin viaduct too – may it never be said, though sometimes it probably is, that I am a photographer only of buses – though the Crumlin shots have yet to appear in print, and perhaps only one of them here, but even while I was then *there* I was aware of highly coloured buses sloping noisily around, and shouldn't I have paid them more attention, only I didn't, and the main thing was those magic pages from ancient copies of the *Railway Magazine* with tales of tramroads hacked out of those barren hillsides by mighty giants who go down in history – take them how you will – as patrons of the arts and oppressors of the poor working man, with their names engraved across the map – or at least the sketch-plan in the RM – for the tramroads they built. Hill, Bailey, and so on. You ain't going to be bothering about buses when you're looking at this much history.

Thus I climbed up Blorenge, one of the finest little mountains in the world, scarred by the incline of the Blaenavon-Abergavenny tramway – up which I was treading from its bottom by the Monmouthshire & Brecon Canal at Llanfoist – and then following it along the more-or-less level round the cap of Blorenge, with most of South Wales or more particularly the Usk Valley and Abergavenny and the Sugar Loaf Mountain and the Brecon Beacons in glorious sunshine spread out before me, possibly the most perfect landscape I have ever beheld anywhere between the Baltic and Braga or Glasgow and

Genova, and what a pity it was, this being Good Friday and me so near to Heaven, that Sweetheart was bound by RC conventions to attend Mass in bungaloid Penarth rather than see the paradise of the high hills . . . for she was convent-educated and her recent preceptresses would not have allowed the notion that you might find more religion in God's good air on a long-abandoned mountainside tramroad than you might in the incense of the Church of Rome (a digression from the course of this tale for which I might apologise, especially as I have muttered about it before in these august pages, were it not that my – or their – these pages' – readers seem to enjoy my repetitions) . . . and then I went back the way I came, down among many stone sleeper blocks (like those referred to earlier; those men of old drilled two holes in a stone to fix their rails) and at the bottom, back in civilisation, a bus hove past, I think it was a Guy utility-bodied, belonging to Heaven-knows-who-long-forgotten, and some lovely Usk nymphs with fluffy outrageous skirts wandered through the foreground, and for what I had shot on the hills above I was out of film, wasn't I!

So tried again, this time with Pontypridd nymphs equally outrageously fluffily skirted, slim-legged among derelict trolleybus poles and some kind of PUDC double-decker; but Sweetheart now again beside me did not really approve and the results were nothing special. *Pudcers* was a nickname employed by my artist friend, who had been brought up there, and possibly by others, to describe the buses of that particular operator in those halcyon pre-classless-society days when old boundaries and civic systems and serfdom yet thrived and every valley had several

now 40 years ago I have some difficulty, except in the case of hymn tunes, in ascribing the place-names to their subjects . . . but I remember that several of these names (though not which ones) decorated the flanks of the buses which, with normal enough names on their always exposed radiators, Leyland and AEC and perhaps (possibly only in my memory or imagination) a preponderance of Guy, appeared by their bodywork often in all conscience foreign enough!

And then, among the sheep, and everywhere, among these buses of many hues, were the buses – ubiquitous, it seemed to me – invariably in red and variously inscribed *South Wales* or *Western Welsh* or *Red & White*. I could not quarrel with the titles but really the buses mostly seemed boring, just tin-front half-cabs, Regent Vs or something like that for the double-deckers, and flat-fronted single-decks such as Tiger Cubs, all far too modern to merit a second glance . . . the sort of buses that when I see one in preservation now it gives a catch to my heart and the memory of how long-lost Sweetheart and I ignored them and I scarcely bothered to photograph them of course, even if I paid some attention to other more exotic specimens . . . On the other hand, obviously Sweetheart and I truly liked and appreciated the Cardiff trolleybuses and more particularly those single-decker trolleybuses and I took a photo of her beside one (to be reproduced herewith, I hope) perhaps to make up for the little angels of Pontypridd . . .

And then there was Newport. Always a bit individual in transport anyway, for it boasted a transporter bridge (and still does, at that, probably a scheduled ancient monument now whether or no it is actually operable) like Middlesbrough, the only other, so far as I know, in GB, and Rouen and Marseille (now late lamented) and Martrou near Rochefort on the Atlantic Coast of France (believed still extant but many years out of use) and the one at Bilbao (or Algorta) Spain, which I hope still flourishes. Newport is a bit special anyway because it is – or was – in Mon (short for Monmouthshire) which was a county never quite sure whether it was in England or Wales and with rules about opening

operators including urban district councils, frequently with vehicles bizarre and unlikely enough to be described as exalted . . . in Cwm Rhondda and places where they sing, anywhere among bleak terraces of miners' terraces stretched along the contours or sometimes almost architecturally impossibly down them, front doors sometimes blocked by stray sheep (live ones in this case) from the barren mountains above. (Once when we were examining a very derelict and unidentifiable but plainly very Western Welsh bus – just another corpse - dumped for no apparent very good reason beside a cottage atop one of the spines between the valleys some specimens of these sheep strayed according to their wont into the middle of the road causing a motor-cyclist to perform dramatic manoeuvres, and, as he got back onto course, to shout to us 'They want all shooting!')

Evocative names

And all this was among evocative names, names of collieries which with gaunt pit-head gear still strove smokingly among the terraces, names of the communities round about them, names of non-conformist hymn tunes written in those places, names of the early railways or tramroads which a century before had served to take the produce from the collieries and ironworks away to wherever they were bound, names like Rassa, Sirhowy, Cwmtillery and Abertillery, Shop Row, Tredegar, Gelligaer, Rhymney, Blaenwern, Pen-y-darren . . . and with all this being

PUDC no.58. Classic basket. Were there a magazine devoted to this subject, this shot should be in it; these baskets were the height of fashion in the late 1950s and evidently still survived in Pontypridd into the early 1960s. The bus is classic too, a 1949 Bristol K5G with Beadle body.

hours of public houses which have now become mere pages of history and CAMRA guide books . . . And apart from this, and never mind about some probably fairly average double-deck buses, it boasted in the early 1960s some pretty strange-looking single-deckers too, full-fronted creatures of attractive bodywork – just as you might likewise say of the Newport nymphs – and something in the back of my mind though possibly erroneously suggests they were Saro. The ultra-knowledgeable Mr Booth is naturally quick to point out that this is indeed erroneous, that they were in fact Dennis Lancet UFs with D J Davies bodies . . . but whatever they were the most interesting thing about them was that despite their up-to-date full fronts they had an open-platform entrance at the rear, as archaic as any Guy Utility! And quite unique to Newport. Mon.

Erratically erotic

And then again much later, or, just to be accurate, in 1986, I was back in Newport and the single-deckers were just as erratically erotic, being Metro-Scanias, lots of them. Or to be precise, according to records from a reliable source, 44 of them. I must now add that Newport also boasted (again from a reliable source) ten Metro-Scania double-deckers, and though I doubtless noticed these too I paid them scant attention, and shall make no further mention of double-deck Metro-Scanias in these words, for it was

the single-deckers on which I was 'hooked'. The reason for this was that in my home town of Winchester, rather more than a dozen years previously, the famous firm of King Alfred in a final flurry of intrepid independence, before fate and the future foreclosed upon it, had indulged in the brave gesture of acquiring three such vehicles (as any bus historian ought very well to know). They were rare enough anywhere else, with somewhere in North London (a place called Stevenage, actually) having four (subsequently in a swap with some fairly awful Leyland Nationals being joined by the King Alfred three,) and London Transport itself having six (one of which went down, perhaps literally, to fame by drowning itself on its first day of service in some lugubrious watery waste known as Clapton Pond) while Manchester had 13 and Liverpool 20 (again, reliable source, thankyou) and in Leicester, the only other fleet I encountered personally, there were 35, and very pretty they were.

Then back where I am supposed to be writing about there was (reliable source) one more, this being

Another PUDC Bristol, an immaculate 1950 L5G/Beadle.

in Pontypridd, though Pontypridd was by this date apparently known as Taff Ely or some such name (with UDCs and serfdom abolished) and had I known it was there I might have tried to chase it up but I didn't and therefore I didn't, but anyway I made the most of the greatest fleet of all which abounded in Newport. They abounded particularly, as might be expected, in the Newport bus station. This time I was not here for Bailey or Hill, I was engaged upon someone else's business and housed in a fairly ghastly motel at said-someone-else's expense somewhere between Newport and Cardiff and had my supper served by an utterly delightful if seriously plump maiden – by name, I gathered, Sarah - with strong Welsh accent who (and which) utterly converted me – by no more, I must hasten to add, than by serving my supper – to the theory that girls who are badly overweight by conventional standards can be as devastatingly attractive as Page 3s . . . just like social blots such as Metro-Metro-Scanias can be. And when I wasn't at supper and not engaged elsewhere I indulged myself in Newport bus station.

Paradise

Newport bus station, hive of Metro Scanias, is, I believe, laid out, along with sundry arts centres and other gems of modern culture, across what was once a very paradise of docks and sidings and lifting bridges serving as the bottom end of many of those gems of railway and canal antiquity straggling down from the hills above. I missed, alas, this earlier form – possibly it had gone even before I had got there in my earliest visits – but the bus station rising phoenix-like on the ruins was bizarre enough with its endless twisting bus shelters over several hundred yards on minor but none-the-less appreciable gradients. Contours . . . nothing to compare with the slopes of Duffryn Crawnon or Blorenge, but perhaps a bit like a *palliasse*.

I spent the rest of my free time in Cardiff bus station which, if it had its charms, was far less winning than Newport, and its buses entirely

modern (though, as I am writing of 1986, I have a horrid sneaking feeling that some might now be allowed in the pages of *Classic Bus*).

Then once again I sought the slopes of Duffryn Crawnon, this time – perhaps 25 years after the first – from the south hitherto forbidden (vaguely though not clearly indicated above) by mining exploits – rather than files of military men! – which were now long abandoned so the southerly or easy approach to Duffryn Crawnon was open; and this time from harmless holiday cottage somewhere near Hay-on-Wye accompanied by new wife and young baby, and not from my palliasse in bungaloid Penarth. Many of those barren slopes were now despoiled (in my view) by Forestry Commission Christmas trees or pines in ranks as serried and sterile as must have been those of the nuns whose teachings had, all those years before, been largely responsible for driving in the wedge which accounted for my final parting from Sweetheart . . . and I could not find the cache where Sweetheart and I had left the other bits of plate-rail . . .

Lost treasures. As lost, as lost forever as all those buses of many colours with unpronounceable but inspiring names. As lost to me as must have been to some hill farmer that dead sheep stretched across a narrow track between a wall of rock and a raging torrent . . .

I might well have finished this essay with the sentence above, save only that even while I was writing it – or in an interval from struggling with same – I discovered in the property pages of the Sunday Times *an advertisement for a cottage for sale in South Wales, and thus feel bound to add a post-script. The cottage was described as near Llangynidir, which (though not a name mentioned*

Newport in Metro-Scania days in 1986. The shelters in Newport bus station seem to sprawl over at least a quarter of a mile, their alignment is by no means straight, and the 'level' of the floor might be likened to a rumpled palliasse.

hitherto in these words) is not far from Duffryn Crawnon, and from the picture I could not tell whether or no it was that same cottage with the 'shell holes' in the roof though it looked pretty similar and was described as being completely derelict, without any 'services', and up a relatively inaccessible track; with several acres of abandoned mountainside attached it was regarded nevertheless as a choice opportunity, and accordingly priced at – if I remember correctly (for I threw the paper away in the meritorious pursuit of preventing the entire house from becoming clogged with unread back-numbers of *Sunday Times* supplements) at either £150,000 or £250,000, with some similar sum required to put it into anything like habitable condition. And even could you render it habitable (though the advertisement did not mention this) you could not – as I saw the proof - send your children to school from it, could you!

The advertisement made no comment about potential proximity to the Bryn Oer Tramroad . . . or its treasures . . . or any remark about responsibility for anything you might find on your several acres such as corpses . . .

No . . . buying this would be the last thing on my mind . . . **CB**

THREE IN A ROW

CHRIS DREW drawings of 666 and 777

666

Don't panic, it's only a number. Leylands here included a Southdown PDI, a Plymouth PD2 and an all-Leyland product for West Riding. Midland Red dropped on to the scene with a real favourite of mine, a BMMO CM6T, whilst Douglas on the Isle of Man brought forth an MCW-bodied Regent V from out of its unusual system. Bradford provided the trolleybus this time and in the drawing is a United Counties Bristol FS. Following close on its heels came Bedford KJS 666 from – oh you fill in the rest!

777

Shall I start this time with the Scottish input? Yes, Glasgow FYS 777 from the small group of Alexander-bodied Sunbeam F4As. Apart from South Yorkshire's experimental bi-modal Dennis, these were the only trolleys ever bodied by that company. More mundane, I better put in GJS 777 from Mitchell's in here as well, and yet another Edinburgh PD2, this one now preserved. East Yorkshire pops in with a Renown modified with its Beverley Bar roof line. Municipalities jump on board with a Maidstone Brush-bodied Daimler CV, a Stockport all-Crossley, and a Manchester, as in the drawing. PMT is represented by a lowbridge Atlantean and the large Dorset independent, Bere Regis, supplied a benchmark vehicle, DDN 777, a Duple Vista-bodied Bedford OB.

TITANS
TAKE OVER

COLIN ROUTH describes West Yorkshire's fleet of Leyland TD1s and TD2s

...est Yorkshire no.403, ...1928 all-Leyland ...tan TD1, in Ilkley ...ound 1932. ...Jackson/C W Routh ...llection

1929 all-Leyland TD1 no.414 at Silsden around 1930 with its driver and flat-capped conductor in attendance.
R Jackson/C W Routh collection

IMAGINE the scene as the Leyland Titan glides away from the stop on its first journey to Skipton, seen off by a group of impressed spectators. No, this is not a cascaded Titan in Stagecoach stripes at Canterbury bus station, nor earlier in London Transport red at Romford, but a quieter version (6.8-litre petrol engine) in the dignified red colours of the West Yorkshire Road Car Company in August 1928.

Like the Arriva companies in 1998, West Yorkshire Road Car Co Ltd had been newly created on 1 January 1928. It was to carry on operations previously marketed as Harrogate & District Road Car Co in the eastern part of the area, Premier Transport Co in the west and Blythe & Berwick at Bradford in the centre. The management was expansionist-minded and aimed at consolidating its area, from Keighley in the west, via Bradford, Leeds and York, to Malton in the east. This, over the next six years, it did, including taking over two municipal operators, Keighley and York.

Eye-catching

The newly-introduced Leyland Titan TD1, with its low height, was not only eye-catching but enabled many operators to provide double-deckers on routes previously inaccessible through the combination of low railway bridges and the very high off-the-ground double-deck format. The Titan met the ever-increasing demand from growing numbers of passengers and helped, urged by Leyland's publicity, to persuade operators to replace their trams with Titans and also to create a network of inter-urban routes. Thus East Kent's were used to improve the links between Canterbury and Dover and Folkestone. West Yorkshire's provided a prestigious route from Bradford through Keighley to Skipton, passing the municipal vehicles of Bradford and Keighley corporations, which could never operate a through service because of the short gap between the ends of their systems, at Cross Flatts and Stockbridge respectively. After 1924 they couldn't be in any case, as Keighley introduced trolleybuses on its section, while Bradford continued and modernised its trams.

Premier Transport had been acquired by Harrogate & District in June 1926 and although it continued to run under its own name, brand-new Tilling-

With the newly-built depot on the right, a TD1 turns at Cunliffe Road, Ilkley. The depot opened in 1928.
R Jackson/C W Routh collection

Stevens B9As identical with those operated by the parent company were soon greatly in evidence. Control of the company was very much from Harrogate, as regular correspondence from the manager revealed to me when I browsed through the file as a company employee much later. All the time the accent was on competition, especially with Keighley Corporation, and it could be that even in 1927 the management had its eye on a possible takeover of that operator, a feat it virtually achieved some five years later. When Keighley-West Yorkshire Services was formed, the Premier manager became depot superintendent at Keighley.

Bible indicators

Six Titans provided the initial service, quickly being joined by another 15 in 1929, all of these being of the more primitive open-staircase format. The 'bible indicator', as it was known, became the standard for West Yorkshire and the first Titans, fitted with the standard Leyland single-line display, were soon refitted with bibles; these indicators got their name from being turned like the pages of a book. This method had the advantage of fitting exactly with the car roster – ie car roster no.21 would have bible indicator no.21, and with one so equipped a driver would have a display for every terminus his vehicle was due to visit that day. Thirteen more Titans arrived in 1930, still with the open-staircase format – a surprising decision this. Keighley Corporation had responded by buying five Titans of its own, but its

old-fashioned-looking trolleybuses were clearly at a disadvantage with the public, and faced with the capital cost of their replacement the council decided to negotiate with the company.

After considering management by a joint committee, it was finally decided to form a new company, Keighley-West Yorkshire Services Ltd, managed by West Yorkshire but with four directors from the company and three from the corporation. The corporation abandoned its trolleybuses on 31 August 1932, leaving it one month to operate buses only until KWY took over. This is where more Titans come into the story.

Piano-fronted

In June 1932 West Yorkshire took delivery of some splendid TD2s, with Eastern Counties bodies which were very modern-looking for the period, having lost the 'piano-fronted' appearance which many bodybuilders, including Leyland, Roe and English Electric, were still using. These six, nos.435-40, were put to work from Keighley depot, one can assume in order to impress Keighley residents with the company's modernity in comparison with their own ageing fleet, to which no new vehicles had been

*Another Cunliffe Road, Ilkley, view, with no.440, a 1932
Eastern Counties-bodied Leyland TD2, passing no.257,
a 1925 Tilling-Stevens B10A2 in 1932.*
R Jackson/C W Routh collection

Above: *Keighley Corporation no.54, a 1928 TD1, at Burlington
Sheds for going-home time in May 1930. In the background are
some of the undertaking's Brush-bodied Straker Squire trolleybuses.
The TD1 became Keighley-West Yorkshire no.K442 in 1932.*
West Yorkshire Information Service

Below: *Well-filled no.437, a 1932 TD2/Eastern Counties, arrives in
New Brook Street, Ilkley, in 1932.*
R Jackson/C W Routh collection

added since the TD1s of 1928. In order to balance the book-keeping involved in setting up KWY Services, no.435 was bought by the corporation on 31 August to run for one month as its no.58, although there is no evidence that 435 showed any change in its outward appearance. It posed for photographs side-by-side with the last trolleybus for the final ceremony.

West Yorkshire no.435 seen in July 1932, when almost new, at Addingham. A TD2/Eastern Counties, it became Keighley Corporation no.58 for the month of September 1932 as part of the deal involving the creation of Keighley-West Yorkshire.
R Jackson/C W Routh collection

Eastern Counties-bodied Titan TD2 no.440 at Cringles, between Addingham and Silsden, when new in 1932.
R Jackson/C W Routh collection

The last corporation manager, Mr H Binns, had served the undertaking well as rolling-stock superintendent and acting manager, and he became depot engineer at Keighley, retiring about the time I joined the company. There were tales about his pipe, which he smoked continually and which was noted for its evil smell. Fitters took bets that he wouldn't tell the difference if horse manure was substituted for tobacco. This was done, and Mr Binns smoked happily on!

When KWY took over operations, its fleet was renumbered in the WY series but with the prefix 'K' added. Seven TD1s were transferred from the WY fleet, including one from the first batch, no.K404. The TD2s remained to operate the ex-trolleybus routes until December when seven similar new TD2s, nos.K446-52, arrived. The WY TD2s then moved on to Leeds and Bradford depots. KWY was given some of WY's services on its formation, including the Ilkley route on which the TD1s had featured. Operation of both KWY and WY services was centred on the WY depot, but careful note of 'contra mileage' was made if a KWY vehicle strayed onto a WY service – or vice versa. (Sometimes this was done to increase or decrease mileage before overhaul.)

Tilling

Only two further TD2s came – nos.K451/2 with Eastern Counties bodies in 1934, accompanied by a pair of Bristol Gs because WY as part of the Tilling empire now had to buy Bristol products. The open-backed TD1s were looking very dated by the mid-1930s but in 1934 WY had taken over York Corporation and operated through a joint committee. Twelve TD1s were drafted in to York to replace York's trams in November, and three more in 1937. This ensured their longer survival; the company's own were withdrawn in 1935 and via a dealer sold to Western SMT. The KWY TD1s, including the former corporation ones, followed in 1938/9, being snapped up by Caledonian Omnibus Company, another Tilling subsidiary.

After the war broke out, the solitary member of the first batch at Keighley, K404, became a tree-lopper, but the war saved YWY's TD1s, as it did in many another fleet. With tram-replacement programmes in deep-freeze, the Titans soldiered on, but not at York. They returned to WY depots, including Leeds and Bradford. At Leeds I occasionally saw Y403, helping out on peak-hour duties, the only open-backed bus in the city, its antediluvian appearance arousing my immediate interest, usually more focussed on the trams. It was not until a visit to London in 1946 that I saw other elderly buses to compare with it, but there at the hub of the Empire were LTs and STs in abundance! WY's open-backed Titans were finally eased out in 1945/6, Y405, the last, surviving until June.

One of the TD2s does survive, of course – or at least partially. It is the famous K451 (JUB 29), an ex-Glasgow TD1 given K451's body by Wallace Arnold

Above: *All except one of the first batch of West Yorkshire TD1s were transferred to York-West Yorkshire in November 1935. No.Y406 is seen at York station around 1938. Note the distinctive 'bible' destination indicator.* The Omnibus Society

Left: *The exhaust of no.439 betrays its diesel engine as it heads through the Hawksworth Estate in Leeds in August 1942. It was on diversion from Kirkstall Road due to flooding. Note the wartime headlamp masks and white edging.* E C Cope, copyright C W Routh

and re-registered at that time. It is well-known at rallies, having been owned by Keith Jenkinson for well over 30 years now.

Finally I should like to acknowledge my indebtedness for some facts in this article to Stanley King's excellent book *Keighley Corporation Transport*, in which more details of abortive negotiations over through-running are mentioned; Keith Jenkinson's history of West Yorkshire Road Car Co, with its fleet details and other information gleaned over the years through the PSV Circle and the West Yorkshire

Ex-Keighley-West Yorkshire K404 after conversion to a tree-lopper, in North's yard in Whinmoor in June 1951.
C W Routh

Information Service. I must also pay tribute to the late Robert Jackson of Silsden, whose photography in the Keighley area in the period 1928-32 did much to illustrate what was going on among WY and its associates at this time. **CB**

WEST YORKSHIRE'S LEYLAND TITANS

Fleet no	Reg no	Chassis/body	New	Withdrawn
401-6	WW 7096-101	TD1/Leyland L27/26RO	1928	1938-46
407-20	WW 7655-8, 8355-64	TD1/Leyland L27/26RO	1929	1937-46
421	WX 329	TD1/Leyland L27/26RO	1929	1937
422-34	WX 2105-17	TD1/Leyland L27/26RO	1930	1937-45
435-40	YG 620-5	TD2/ECOC L26/26R	1932	1948/9
K441-5	WW 7422, 5510, 7861-3	TD1/Leyland L27/24RO	1928	1938/9
K446-52	YG 2053-9	TD2/ECOC L26/26R	1932	1947/8
K453/4	YG 5731/2	TD2/ECOC L26/26R	1934	1948

Transferred to Keighley-West Yorkshire 2/10/32: 404/14-7/9/20, 435*
Transferred to York-West Yorkshire 27/11/35: 401-3/5-13
Transferred to York West Yorkshire 1/11/37: 430/2/3

*This had been owned by the corporation for the previous month

All TD2s were fitted with Gardner oil engines in the mid-1930s; K453/4 arrived with them

Born: Derby, 31 October 1913

Parents: British Automobile Traction and Commercial Car Hirers. BAT, the bus-operating wing of British Electric Traction, was keen to establish services where BET didn't already run trams, so used Trent to expand into Derbyshire and Nottinghamshire. CCH was the transport-operating subsidiary of the manufacturer then called Commercial Cars, later better known as Commer. Just as Leyland had bus-operating interests, Commer recognised that it could sell more buses and lorries if it operated some of them itself. CCH built up a small network of services around Derby between 1909 and 1913, and had six Commers when Trent was established.

How long did the joint venture last?: Over nine years, during which period CCH was responsible for day-to-day management. CCH sold out from January 1923 and Trent came under full BAT ownership until 1928, when it became part of the newly created Tilling & BAT. Tilling didn't own any shares in Trent, but the following year saw the LMS and LNER railway companies buy into Trent.

Presumably it stopped buying Commers?: That stopped early on in the joint venture, when Maudslay, Tilling-Stevens, Thornycroft and Daimler became its most popular makes. But BAT ownership saw some in-house purchasing.

What was that?: There was a particularly close relationship with the larger neighbouring BAT company to the west, Midland Red. They shared a chairman, and Midland Red's legendary traffic manager, O C Power, was a Trent director from 1923 until his death 20 years later. The upshot of this was that Trent bought large numbers of Midland Red's home-made SOS-type buses in the 1920s and at various times during the 1930s, although AECs and Daimlers became increasingly popular through the 1930s. Postwar purchasing, when Trent once again was a BET company, was mainly a mix of Leylands and AECs, with the Daimler Fleetline finding favour after Leyland bought AEC. Among its most notable buses was the very last Leyland-bodied bus – one of six PD2/12s – delivered in December 1954.

Other notable vehicles: Twenty Willowbrook-bodied 1946/7 AEC Regal halfcabs were lengthened in 1958 and converted from 35- to 39-seaters with full fronts slightly similar to those on contemporary Tiger Cubs.

Who owned Trent next?: Following the sale of BET's British bus interests in March 1968, Trent became part of the National Bus Company on its formation in 1969. This led to big changes three years later.

What were they?: In January 1972 Trent took over management of the neighbouring Midland General and Notts & Derby companies, which had been in state ownership since 1948 and were part of the Balfour Beatty group before that. Notts & Derby was turned into a property-owning company and Midland General was fully absorbed into Trent four years later. As if that wasn't enough, Trent also fell heir to North Western Road Car's Peak District operations – run out of Buxton and Matlock depots – in March 1972, following the sale of the Greater Manchester routes to SELNEC PTE.

And when NBC was sold off?: Trent's management, operating by the name of Wellglade, bought it in December 1986 and

CHECK POINT

No.4: Trent Motor Traction

unusually has retained the business ever since. It has even reactivated Notts & Derby as an operating company, and the main business now trades as Trent Barton, reflecting its biggest acquisition, in 1989. Not that this was the first time Trent had thought of buying Barton.

When was that?: October 1921. David Bean, who has so far produced two volumes of an intended four-part work on Trent's history, says Barton wanted £25,000 for a business that then ran 25 buses, but Trent was only prepared to pay £13,000. A year later, Barton hoped to get a better deal out of Trent's bigger brother by seeking £30,000 from Midland Red. Unsurprisingly, that got it nowhere, but Trent did later buy a shareholding in Barton that didn't pass to Wellglade upon privatisation.

Any other acquisitions?: There were many small companies, like Dutton's Unity Service of Nottingham and Daley of Ripley (both 1935) and Naylor of South Normanton (1956), but two turned-down postwar opportunities are probably of greater interest. Trent declined to buy Stevensons of Uttoxeter and Gash of Newark. The course of British bus industry would have been quite different had it taken up either option, and especially that to buy Stevensons when its owner died.

Livery?: Most buses were green from CCH days up to 1923, when a BET red, said then to be the same as Midland Red's, was adopted. This was relieved by white and, sometimes, dark red. Postwar colours were light red and cream (coaches were dark red), but a 1957/8 experiment saw some buses painted all-red (again like Midland Red), before a cream band was added. Livery soon reverted to equal areas of red and cream. But the NBC era ushered in poppy red and a white band from 1972. Wellglade ownership has brought about a great variety of post-classic liveries.

Alan Millar

Trent bought typical BET-group fare in the 1960s. This Leyland Leopard PSU3/1R with Marshall body was new in 1964.
Michael Dryhurst

THE WAY T

Photos taken by JOHN ROBINSON 30 years ago

Above: *In 1965/6 Eastern National converted a number of 1953 Bristol KSW5Gs with ECW lowbridge bodywork to open-top layout. Among them was WNO 482, pictured in Sheringham on 19 August 1973 in the ownership of Culling's, Norwich. Although it was 20 years old it looked immaculate in Culling's distinctive grey, yellow and cream livery.*

Left: *Numerically the first Bristol VRT delivered new to Eastern Counties was VR365, dating from 1969. It is depicted in Thorpe Road, Norwich, heading towards the city centre on 17 August 1973 in full pre-NBC red/cream livery. This photo, like all John's photos taken before 3 September 1973, were taken on a Kodak Retina 35mm camera; after that date he used a Zenit B. At that time only standard lenses were used.*

Previous page: *Heading along Southport's genteel Lord Street on 27 October 1973 is one of the corporation's then almost-new Alexander-bodied Leyland Atlanteans, no.85, one of ten delivered that year. These replaced 1952-vintage Weymann-bodied Leyland PD2/12s and were the first (and only) rear-engined double-deckers purchased before the corporation was absorbed into Merseyside PTE on 1 April 1974, along with similarly-liveried St Helens Corporation. John Robinson liked the buses so much that 28 years later he bought similar no.89 and returned it to the condition represented by no.85.*
All photos by John Robinson

Top: *Ribble purchased a batch of 105 Leyland Titan PD3/4 with full-fronted Burlingham bodywork in 1957/8. One of these, no.1512, is seen on driver training duties in St Helens on 27 July 1973 as it turns into Shaw Street from Hall Street. A St Helens Corporation AEC Swift follows close behind and more St Helens buses can be seen parked opposite the undertaking's Hall Street garage. Apart from a single body built on Guy Arab IV for Wolverhampton Corporation, this type of bodywork was unique to Ribble.*

Above: *Many operators began to discover the financial appeal of overall advertisements in the early 1970s. PMT was no exception, and this Leyland Atlantean with semi-lowbridge Weymann bodywork, no.797, received this basically white scheme for London & Manchester Assurance. This was among PMT's first batch of Atlanteans new in 1959 and originally with fleetnumbers L9766-9800. It is seen in Ironmarket, Newcastle-under-Lyme, on a scorching 16 June 1973, evidenced by the open entrance doors.*

SELNEC PTE inherited two batches of Leyland Atlanteans with Liverpool-style Metro-Cammell bodywork from Bolton Corporation in 1969, together with a batch from Bury Corporation. As these two views show, there were significant differences between the Bolton batches. The first seven, nos.6693-9, new in 1963 and represented by the first photo, were more or less pure Liverpool-style apart from the Bolton destination indicators and flat windscreen. They were the only Atlanteans delivered to Bolton with an open cutaway above the engine compartment, instead of engine shrouds. The second batch of eight, nos.6719-26, dated from 1965 and incorporated standard Bolton features like engine shrouds, polished metal trims on the lower panels and squarer wheelarches. The buses were photographed on 13 October 1973 on consecutive frames of film, travelling in opposite directions in Blackhorse Street, Bolton, alongside the town's Moor Lane bus station.

Top: *Liverpool Corporation got more involved with single-deck one-man operation than any major UK city outside London when, in 1968/9, it took delivery of 110 Leyland Panthers with Metro-Cammell bodywork. Originally delivered in a reversed livery of cream with green window surrounds to signify the need to pay fares to the driver, the livery was later reversed again to that shown on no.1085, seen running into Liverpool city centre from Norris Green on 17 November 1973. The Panthers proved to be unreliable vehicles, a situation experienced by many other operators of the model, and almost half of the Liverpool fleet was out of service by 1975, either withdrawn or sold.*

Above: *The break-up of North Western in 1972 saw its Buxton and Matlock garages, together with their vehicles and services, pass to Trent. Visually not dissimilar to some of North Western's own vehicles is this indigenous Trent Leyland Tiger Cub with BET-style Alexander bodywork, no.180, one of a batch of 20 new in 1962. When photographed in Buxton on 3 September 1973, operating former North Western service 85 to Glossop, it had been transferred to Buxton garage and still wore full pre-NBC livery.*

Top: *AEC Regents first appeared in the Morecambe & Heysham fleet in 1932 and, apart from five Leyland Titans delivered in the early 1960s, all buses purchased up to 1970 were of AEC manufacture. A number of the 1949 batch of Regent IIIs were later converted to open-top, the attractive lines of their Park Royal bodywork disfigured by plywood advertising boards as shown by no.64 on Morecambe's promenade on 1 August 1973, heading for Heysham Village.*

Above: *Early in 1972 South Wales Transport took over the Neath and Haverfordwest depots of Western Welsh along with their services and 57 vehicles. Among the buses transferred was no.338, formerly Western Welsh no.1384, a 1966 Leyland Tiger Cub with dual-purpose bodywork by Marshall, depicted in Tenby on 22 September 1973. With the transfer around the same time to Crosville of WW's services in Cardiganshire, South Wales operated entirely to the west of Western Welsh!*

Top: *In the 1970s John Robinson's school journey from Knutsford to Wilmslow was provided by Godfrey Abbott Group, Sale, using a mix of coaches, generally purchased new, and secondhand buses – both single- and double-deck. Rear-engined double-deckers first appeared in the fleet in 1972 and among them were two Leyland Atlanteans new in 1960 to Gateshead & District; these had Alexander bodywork of the original style fitted to Atlantean chassis. KCN 182, wearing GAG's livery of mustard and olive green, heads empty down Adams Hill past Knutsford railway station shortly after the start of the new school term in September 1973. In November 1976 the operator was taken over by Greater Manchester PTE.*

Above: *In 1961 North Western took delivery of 20 AEC Reliance coaches with Alexander bodywork, nos.832-51. These were later downgraded to buses as depicted by no.838 leaving Altrincham bus station on the local service to Halebarns on 24 July 1973. Although retaining North Western livery, the bus was by then operating with SELNEC's Cheshire division, which had taken over a large part of North Western the previous year. The brown 'CHESHIRE' symbol is barely visible above the front wheelarch in this view; more usually on buses that had not yet been painted in SELNEC's orange/white livery it was placed on a white panel for greater legibility.*

Top: *Lincolnshire Road Car was the largest operator of the lightweight Bristol SC4LK, taking a total of 113 between 1956 and 1961. Although only developing 57bhp at 2100rpm from the 3.8-litre Gardner 4LK engine, this was adequate for the largely flat terrain in which they operated. In this view at Holbeach garage on 20 August 1973 one of the 1959 batch, no.2471, stands ahead of Bristol VRT no.1905. Both buses, of course, carry ECW bodywork.*

Above: *Climbing Derby Street, Bolton, on 13 October 1973, is Lancashire United 'jumbo' Daimler Fleetline no.396. One of a batch of ten new in 1972, half had dual-doorway Northern Counties bodywork, as shown here, and the other half had single-door bodies. These buses introduced a broad grey band between decks, although this wasn't applied retrospectively to any other double-deckers apart from six broadly similar 'jumbos' in 1970/1.*

THREE IN A ROW

The final selection of CHRIS DREW drawings, as he reaches 999

888

Kent produced three vehicles on its own – East Kent's Park Royal-bodied Guy Arab IV and Maidstone & District's Bristol K and all-Leyland PD2. Yorkshire came second with a Leeds Regent V and West Riding Guy Wulfrunian (drawing). Lincolnshire Road Car gave me a natty Bristol SC while the other side if the country saw two lowheight types appear: a Dennis Loline III/Alexander from North Western and a rather ungainly Bridgemaster for South Wales. Meanwhile back at the ranch, who else? GJS 888 – the usual, from Mitchell's.

999

I felt like ringing this number by now, and asking them to please come and take me away. But, dear reader, I carried on to the bitter end. By the way, if you don't believe any of this, the information is there – go and find it. Back to business. The South of England came up trumps with these numbers: Brighton, Hove & District with a Bristol K and KSW, Maidstone a Massey-bodied PD2, Maidstone & District an ECW-bodied Bristol L. Western National brought forth a standard Bristol K and Black & White came on board with a Willowbrook-bodied Royal Tiger. Portsmouth produced three by itself: a Leopard, (in drawing), a PD2 and a PD3, all with Weymann bodywork. In the Midlands, Barton threw up a Duple Firefly-bodied Bedford. Lancashire towns were represented by (a) Liverpool with a Regent III/Crossley and (b) Ramsbottom with an all-Leyland Royal Tiger. Over the Pennines, Bradford could humm up a trolley. Going further on north, Edinburgh let slip a PD3 with Alexander bodywork. If at this point you are waiting for me to give me another entry from Mitchell's, well, I'm sorry, I can't. I've checked the books and I have drawn (excuse pun) a blank. That is unless – as has been oft written in this and like publications – someone out there knows better ...

ROGER AND OUT

Former busman, ROGER DAVIES, discovers Sheffield

'NO.' It turned out to be a short, sharp and absolutely correct answer. It was emitted by Harold E Davies OBE, headmaster of Canton High School for boys at some dire point in the summer of 1968 when we were considering A-level results. I had asked whether my three rather dismal grades were sufficient for the two very generous ones offered by Queen's Belfast to do Geography. Whereas, at the time, I may have felt the Monarch's honour stood for Orrible Bloomin' 'Edmaster, as always, the HM delivered. He was absolutely right, and good thing too.

There's a few reasons for this. I'd missed the trolleybuses and the situation in Belfast in late 1968 may not have been to my taste. To make matters worse, I'd gone off Geography bigtime. Unknown then, another factor played its part. Later, a friend and I hitched around Denmark. At each hostel we were followed by a very dull boring character who would have been on my course in Belfast had I got there. All in all, a lucky escape.

Do you know that at that time of said hitch, Odense Bytraffik worked a fantastic, simple, easy driver-only system on its elderly maroon-and-white Volvo buses? You boarded at the back and the bus was equipped with change machines. As you left at the front, you put the correct fare into a box by the driver. Brilliant! Kobenhaven Sporvege still had one tram route, the 5, worked by Düwag cars which later went to Egypt, and the Aarhus system was still working. This comprised two routes, one going to the incredibly English Dalgas Avenue, with both starting at Marienlund. Here was the Youth Hostel and, one night, I led a party back after a night of some alcohol to celebrate a guy from Thunder Bay

Above: *Railway influence in the Sheffield 'C' fleet and here's an ECW-bodied Leopard at Pond Street bus park in July 1969. A bit of a Burlingham-bodied one is on the left. The railway influence stretched to the 'B' fleet, which had similar motors, but not the 'A' fleet. No.3080, one of only nine buses new in 1961, passed to NBC the year after this photo when the joint committee was wound up.* All photos by Roger Davies

Left: *Local-authority indulgence, part one. This Cravens-bodied Bedford bought in 1966 and numbered 1 was apparently for use by the Sheffield Corporation Transport Committee. Goodness knows how this came about, but what a simply staggering bus to find in a major municipal fleet. But here in October 1971 we catch them out and it's working a Bamford short on route 44. The 44, along with the 37, 40 and 72, provided the good folk of Sheffield with a pretty comprehensive service into the delightful Peak District.*

Local-authority indulgence, part two. This 1958 Roe-bodied Reliance really was for the Transport Committee although it was available for private hire. Again, what a splendid thing to find in a big municipality – and look at the superb registration, which would be worth more than the coach now. There's really not a lot more to say except that Leeds had one too . . .

Ontario's birthday. I simply followed the tramlines – you don't get that in the pre-qualifying bids, do you? Wasn't exactly direct, but we got there and, as it was well past curfew, climbed through a window and over the bunk of a sleeping Eskimo. He loved his Vodka and made sure he shared it with the Yungenherbergsvater (as the Germans would have it) so we all slept in until 10.30. Not very YHA at all.

Crikey, where are we going? Well, I certainly wasn't going to Belfast so I went to Greyfriars Road in Cardiff instead. This was quite an important corporation bus terminus but was home to services I had no need to use. Weird isn't it, when you see familiar buses that whisk you home with all sorts of different numbers and destinations? Well, I think so. Here were to be found, amongst others, 25s to Rhiwbina, 27s to Templeton Avenue and 34s to Caldy Road. I once caught a 25, worked by the hotpants conductress (if you don't read *Classic Bus*, you can't hope to keep up) who was operating her 'flat fare of the day' system. Anyway, I don't suppose I looked at the buses that day, as a crisis loomed: I may become a Third Year Sixth. I had seen these wraith-like creatures drifting along the school corridors in uniforms clearly past their withdraw-by date. Bit like Cardiff's trams, trolleybuses and Alexander Arab Vs. This was not for me so I was headed

for the education offices. Initially, my lack of a foreign-language O-level was a stumbling block but suddenly my guide lit up and asked: 'Have you ever considered Public Administration at Sheffield?' The correct answer was no I hadn't. I had thought about Sheffield – that's where some buses that passed my relatives in Bradford's house went as you saw in Yearbook 8. You really should do some research before you start reading these things. Not a lot of people had thought of Public Administration, though, for it was a brand-new course put on with admirable foresight by the Polytechnic, in anticipation of what was to become the 1972 Local Government Act. This Act had even more impact on me in later life with the responsibilities it gave Local Councils over bus services and subsidies. (Look, OK, it was still the College of Technology then but was becoming a Poly and we were its first BA course; until then it had specialised in BSc in bricklaying and that sort of thing.) A phone call elicited an application and date for interview, and within days I was emerging from Sheffield Midland to a sea of cream-and-blue buses. Let's be clear about this: I was drinking at the Last Chance Saloon, there were no wheels on my wagon, this was the final place the UK Higher Education system had for me. I was petrified.

Look, I know about reliability and all that, but these were seriously smart functional buses. Park Royal Swift no.29 is here just before Christmas in 1971 working the City Clipper service. This was a classic tale of local politics. Sheffield Transport had been obliged to make some quite severe service cuts which, even at my early stages of bus understanding, I could see had been well thought-out, if painful. Then Leeds starts up a city centre service using Mercedes minibuses and the local politicians in Sheffield jump up and say 'We must have one too!' Enter City Clipper, which lost just about the same amount of money as had been saved in the service cuts. The Swifts probably appreciated it though; Sheffield started to sell them off very quickly and the 500 probably saved a number of them.

So I bus-spotted. Well, come on – it was like a security blanket. Later, those with a feel for chronology asked awkward questions about the blue lines in the Sheffield fleet in my BBF2. It was about this time I started to put about the theory that you can rightly 'cop' a bus if you see it on the TV or in a film. (This is clearly preposterous; it's like saying you've visited a country if you merely change planes there.) Anyway, after a nasty moment with a fried egg, I tipped up for the interview and at the end, the chairman offered me a place. I was so overwhelmed I just sat there. 'You can say yes now, if you want to,' he said. (He turned out to be an inveterate gambler; I once won his wife and her horse, in that order, at a game of tiddlywinks. Well, I was Sheffield champion, which makes my poor second in the Halki, Greece, World Championships in 2002 all the harder to bear.) I like to think his gamble on me paid off.

For me it did; for starters there was Sheffield Transport. Now those of you who have done some research and not just leapt blindly into this will have come across my comments about how boring the buses were in London and Birmingham. Whilst mildly provocative, I really mean this. Growing up in Cardiff with its multiplicity of different bus companies running in, I can't see how a very dominant operator with hordes of buses the same can be of much interest. (People who can tell a Park Royal RT from a Weymann one bother me slightly; I can tell a Cravens one, but who can't?) You can probably hazard a guess about my views of the present day. Sheffield was something else. Here was a

genuinely dominant operator providing not only the city services but suburban and quite a lot of long-distance ones too. Had they had a standard Sheffield bus it would have been truly awful. But they didn't, they had all sorts of stuff, lots of it what I would call territorial operator kit, which in a way they were. They had big batches of some things, 30s, 40s, so you could see a lot the same and small batches and individual buses so there was lots of variety. With a fabulous operating area, it was just about my ideal operator. If they'd adopted the all-over green livery tried in the early 1950s, they would have been my number one. Incidentally, the reason they didn't was that it was too like arch-rival Leeds. I need make no comment about the present situation. The transport department hadn't anticipated this and had stockpiled green paint which is why street-light poles in Sheffield were green for many years.

So how come the corporation ran over such a huge area? If it's a bit odd you can guarantee the railways must be mixed up in it somewhere. I like to imagine the scene where the wagon-train scout comes over a hill and discovers Sheffield. I loved that TV show *Wagon Train* and always wanted to be the scout, a fearless cove called Flint McCullough. He used to scout ahead then go back and tell the wagon master (can't remember his name, but he was played by Ward Bond) what lay ahead. So Flint tips up and says to Ward (well, whatever his name was): 'Huge city ahead and no buses.' Well, I like to dwell on such nonsense . . . Flint . . . honestly!

This is a Regent III with tin front and Roe body dating from 1955. No.1266 is here newly painted but minus fleetnames in May 1969 at Campo Lane, one of a number of city-centre termini that warranted the general description of 'City'. It may be that something was afoot with the impending ending of the Joint Committee, for this was a 'B' fleet bus; in any case, a smart new fleetname style in blue was about to appear. The 'A' fleet had similar motors and it was usual to have similar types in the three fleets with widely varying fleetnumbers.

Anyway here's Sheffield, growing like the clappers but with no territorial bus company or railway company really being able to lay claim to it. So the LNER and LMS approached the corporation and the Sheffield Joint Omnibus Committee was born. Services within the city were the 'A' fleet, solely the corporation's bit; long stuff to the likes of Manchester and Gainsborough was the 'C' fleet, the railway's bit; and those in-between the 'B' fleet, with costs and revenues shared. The fleet ultimately had a standard livery and buses mixed on work although 'C' buses tended to be more luxuriously appointed for the longer work. The relevant letter was carried below the fleetnumber, and by the time I got there separate fleetnumber schemes were in force. The 'A's went up to 1000 (993 if you want to be picky), the 'B's were 1000s and 2000s (why, as there were a lot less of them?) and the 'C's 3000s, reaching the dizzy heights of 3165. This was heady stuff.

And what buses. We've already touched on exposed-radiator Regent Vs and later tin-front Regent IIIs (look, the captions in Yearbook 7 got confused – OK?). There was a predominance of Regents and Titans both long and short, with Roe and MCW bodies and the one unusual batch of Alexander 30ft Regent Vs. A small clump of Bridgemasters arrived – five quite sleek 30ft rear-entrance ones and one box-on-wheels forward-entrance job. There were some early Atlanteans and three Fleetlines and, despite contemporary adverts intimating that these were single-handedly responsible for replacing trams, the Regents and Titans did most of the work.

A word about trams. It was a mere eight years after their departure that I arrived, and the city clearly still mourned their passing. It is no surprise to me that Sheffield was quick off the mark with a new tramway. You could still buy the commemorative brochure in the SCTD office in Castle Square ('The Hole In The Road') and I duly, if somewhat puzzledly, did. (There's a lot I can't forgive Sheffield Supertram for, but the destruction of the dramatic, space-age sheer self-confident symbolism of Castle Square is my tops.)

Back to buses, and the railway involvement allowed such oddities as ECW-bodied Leopards and PD2s. Following a brief flirtation with some rather fine forward-entrance Regents with Park Royal and MCW bodies, Sheffield went rear-engined bigtime.

About that time, quite a number of fleets rebelled against the style of early rear-engined types. Granted, some were pretty terrible – Sheffield had some early Roes that are best forgotten – but the original MCW style wasn't that bad and with a bit of judicious fiddling, like Manchester did, you got a pleasant and, here comes my point, timeless bus. The trouble with some of the early dramatic experiments was that they looked stunning when new but dated quickly.

Away from the dark satanic mills vision of Sheffield, Regent V no.803 in July 1969 at the Rivelin Dams terminus of the hourly 54. From here it was a delightful walk across the dam and up through Forestry Commission pathways to Lodge Moor and the every-12-minutes 51. Even better was to walk down from Lodge Moor and await the 54 in the comfort of the Norfolk Arms, purveyors of the fine Tetley bitter. There's a tale to be told about buses and pubs – I must get round to it. Anyway, this shows the huge variety in Sheffield's operating area.

Later, bodybuilders, Park Royal in particular, built modern, classic timeless designs, but in the mid-1960s a bit of thrashing about went on. I'd put the so-called Sheffield style of Park Royal body into this category. And it was not as one would have believed. To the outside world, they were Atlanteans and 1964 show exhibit no.340, complete with badge above the rear lower-deck windows, was indicative of teeming hordes. Well, no, not really. The first 30 and second 25 of the body style were all Fleetlines and the remainder of 340's batch of 21 Atlanteans had Neepsend bodies. In 1966 it really got underway with the aforementioned teeming hordes, although a sizeable chunk of those had Neepsend bodies too, so variety was intact. (As an aside, local enthusiasts had names for various types, and the Park Royal Atlanteans were known as 'Gibbons', becoming 'Stuffed Gibbons' when converted for driver-only operation.)

So, all turned out in the distinctive 'it could only be Sheffield' (but seriously impractical) cream-with-three-blue-bands livery, sporting a tidy underlined fleetname, this was the fleet that greeted me 12 years to the day before coach deregulation and my launch of Invictaway. But dramatic change foreshadowed in the 1968 Show was about to occur. Having settled into Mrs Rutkowski's college-approved digs ('I have plenty room', she was Italian married to a Polish steelworker), I set off, David Attenborough-like, into the dark city to track down my prey. And at Bridge Street bus station I found it. Quietly shimmering in brand-new paint, its huge 33ft length exaggerated by the small confines of its perch, stood no.194, a dual-door monster of Park Royal and Leyland parentage. I'd never seen anything like it. '10 Parson Cross' it proclaimed, so thence, in the dark, I went. Although crew-operated, the centre doors were being used for leaving, and at some point I felt that I should try it out and get a bus back. Behind me came an aged chap with a walking stick. The doors shut and 194 set off, walking stick still embedded in the centre door and aged chap showing an admirable turn of speed in pursuit. I don't think centre-door buses ever had a chance with me after that.

Mrs Rut's was just off Abbeydale Road, and here's another of those things that makes classic bus enthusiasm what it is. As a sensible operator – you know, all grown up, long trousers and all that – it makes sense to group route numbers so folk can easily identify their bus. But as an enthusiast it's terrific to have nonsense, so we could catch a 1, 17, 24 or 63, or, wait for it, a 45 and pay one penny extra! Now I'm guessing here, but I reckon the 45 was a 'B' fleet route so you got protection even though it was the same operator! And what destinations: the 1 went to Dobcroft Road, the 17 to Bradway, the 24 to Millhouses, the 63 to Greenhill and the 45 to Totley, Cross Scythes. Added to all this there were three different ticket systems, Ultimate, Setright and TIM. Again, it may be the three different fleets, but the Setrights seemed dominant. Maybe some ticket expert out there can help.

So here we had a city fleet that could take you well out into the countryside. This applied not only to the obvious long-distance routes but to local ones too. Some, like said 45, had odd extensions beyond the

Railway influence again and 'C' fleet no.3153 is a KSW-style ECW-bodied Leyland Titan PD2. In April 1970 it is in Pond Street bus station working city service 46 to Darnall, a regular haunt. This seems a very late use of a 'C' fleet bus, suggesting they weren't all withdrawn at once. You can see here the refinement of platform doors.

regular terminus, in this case Owler Bar, and others like the 18 to Oughtibridge were really rural routes. I used the latter for my few attempts at sailing, always a show-stopper, that, sailing in Sheffield! (It was on Damflask reservoir.) But some truly city services did too, like the 51 to Lodge Moor from which remote terminus you could amble out on to the moors and, if you timed it right, walk down to get a 54 back from Rivelin Dams. Of course, Sheffield still had its heavy industry, but this tended to be concentrated in the Don valley towards Rotherham. I remember peering over a railway bridge into Brown Bailey's steelworks and seeing steam trains, steam cranes and steam lorries still at work in 1968! The southern part of the city was pleasantly tree-lined, suburban and given to steep hills, earning Sheffield the title of England's biggest village. It was here that most student digs were to be found, and most students of the day will recall 81, 82 and 88 buses up the Eccleshall Road and the classic student route, the 60 to Crimicar Lane via many halls of residence. The 60 started at Midland Station across the road from the bus station, maybe because so many students arrived laden with baggage !

I recall using an Eccleshall Road bus one night, returning the then current girlfriend to her residence. She was going on at length about her friend who was dating a builder who had a car. As we left the bus, I pointed to the front and said: 'Look,

I've brought you home in a Daimler.' Didn't wash.

A Sheffield quirk was that destinations into the city centre showed 'City', which, as there were a number of termini dotted about, was probably a good idea. It's funny what impressions the uninitiated, the non-bus enthusiast gets of buses. You've probably gathered I found Sheffield destinations fascinating but it was some years in that I mentioned the 95 terminus of 'Intake' to a fellow student. 'Is that a place?' quoth he; 'I thought it was a description, you know, like Special or Private'. One basic rule of studenthood that I learned early on was 'never spend your birthday in College'. I applied that rigidly but forgot the subsidiary rule 'nor your friends' either'. After ensuring the well-being of the local Stones brewery one lunchtime on such an occasion, I felt the need to go home. I caught the bus and to attempt some contact with reality, concentrated on its fleetnumber on the inside of the front dome. The conductor arrived and enquired about my requirements. '826', I bellowed to his amusement. (OK, save you rooting about, it was a Roe PD2.)

But what of impressions? I must say I thought they were pretty good, but I never felt they had a good relationship with the local *Star* newspaper. The livery was very original and I think people appreciated it, but, by heck, did it get dirty! It is beyond comprehension how the dreadful SYPTE livery ever came about, given the strong identities

that made it up. But one incident in the press made it as an item in one of our lectures in college and became a guiding principle for me throughout my career. A lady had complained to the *Star* that she had been waiting for a relatively infrequent bus (the half-hourly 50 to Dore). It arrived in darkness, and an inspector hopped off and sent the bus away empty. She enquired if that meant she had to wait for the next one to which he implied it was a free country. Now, we all know what happened: the bus was late and was sent light to get back on time. It happens; if you get caught out, simple: you grovel. This was taken up by the paper with a Bus Chief who said (and I quote): 'This is perfectly correct, the bus had a schedule to keep to it didn't have time to pick up passengers.' I never ever forgot that the only reason for running buses was to pick up passengers.

In 1970 interest was reduced when the joint committee was wound up. The corporation took over the 'B' fleet, giving it another opportunity for one of its favourite pastimes, renumbering. The entire 'C' fleet was withdrawn and

an NBC subsidiary called Amalgamated Passenger Transport (APT) set up to take it over. The routes went to surrounding NBC companies and the fleet spread around, mainly to Yorkshire Woollen District. APT itself had an interesting life, ending up, I think, running Lincolnshire's central works. So another quirky, interesting but important part of British transport history came to an end.

Sheffield built up a huge fleet of big two-door Atlanteans; then, with a change of general manager, went back to Fleetlines and single doors. Driver-only operation spread quickly, so riding the last crew operation became a regular sport. This too reduced interest, as anything tended to turn up on Sheffield's routes, but after driver-only it could only be buses so fitted. Atlanteans returned to favour but the last new buses before I left were East Lancs-bodied Bristol VRs delivered in place of Pennine-bodied Bristol REs. Sheffield had gone off long singles, and the exchange rate for 22 REs was 18 VRs. Pennine didn't do doubles though, so East Lancs got the job. It was a

Park Royal went on to build the huge 33ft dual-door Atlanteans that so symbolised Sheffield of the 1970s. At first the design didn't really work too well, and the narrow windscreen gave them a decidedly old-fashioned look. Later ones had a deep screen, which improved them no end and one of each is here at Bridge Street bus station, site of my first encounter with such things. No.207 with the shallow screen is an 'A' fleet bus and no.1142 with the deep screen and improved destination layout is a 'B' – both are on the same route though. Shortly afterwards, the absorption of the 'B' fleet and the need to make room for lots more of these, resulted in them being renumbered 607 and 742 respectively. Park Royal also removed the peaks, although not for Sheffield, and devised one of the all-time classic UK bus designs.

fitting end really, for some years later at M&D we bought 12 of those VRs.

Well, team, I was going to tell you about all the other operators in Sheffield but have got carried away and gone mad with photos too. Despite the dominant status of Sheffield Transport, there were lots of others about: NBCs like Yorkshire Traction, Yorkshire Woollen, West Riding, East Midland, Mexborough & Swinton, Trent and North Western; municipals like Chesterfield, Rotherham, Huddersfield and Doncaster; and independents such as Booth & Fisher, Dearneways and Wigmores. There's so much more to tell. So, was Sheffield in the late 1960s interesting?

Yes.

Routes out of Sheffield in 1969.